The Fish Club

D0731577

they left their nets

a vision for community ministry

w. graham pulkingham

Distributed by
LOGOS INTERNATIONAL
Plainfield, New Jersey

*by special arrangement with
the Publisher*

MOREHOUSE-BARLOW CO.
NEW YORK

Copyright © 1973
by
Morehouse-Barlow Co., Inc.
14 East 41st Street
New York, New York 10017

SBN: 0-8192-1156-7
Library of Congress Catalog Card No.: 73-84091

Printed in the United States of America

seeds of war and seeds of peace
by martha keys

peace, peace, there is no peace
we've cried, we've tried
we cannot find it
not just the peace that glows inside:
for that we have the power
in a flower or a little weed
i can find the peace i need inside
where is the peace
that can free me not to hide from you
fearing to be found?

i see you coming down the street
paralyzed by fear of meeting
another barricaded face
i pass by
on the other side
i return to the fear
i've learned
to live and sleep and breathe

peace, peace, there is no peace
we've cried, we've tried
we cannot find it

we are whirling silences
touching circumferences
retreating
into our own orbits
we return
to the fear we've learned
to live and sleep and breathe

we need a strong peace
not a treaty
to keep us each
on our side of the line
we need a peace that flows between us
giving me to you
and you to me
we need a very gentle peace
that reaches back
to when we were children:
peace that touches us
when we were hurt
and couldn't cry
and when we cried
and no one came
peace that holds us
till we are loved free
of all the aching memories
that make me afraid of you
and you of me

we need a strong peace
breaking down the wall that stands between us
stone and cold and overgrown
with ancient vines
choking hope

we need the bond of peace:
unbreakable
unshakable fact:
me given to you
you given to me

we are one
the old walls fall
the old hurts heal

war-weary world
come
and see
maybe our lives can be a sacrament
love's presence in a world that's bent
the first foothold on the way to hope

we have learned to repent
not just relent
from doing what we want to do:
you hurting me
me hurting you
we've turned
touched each other
and we see
we are one
i am part of you
you're part of me

war-weary world
if only you can see
we live at peace
maybe the hope you've held inside
afraid to breathe
afraid to quench the fragile candle flame
that flickered in the fury
of the war storm

maybe you could begin to breathe
maybe you could begin to believe
peace can be as strong
as the killing and the wrong
we all have lived and died through
maybe you could see enough
to seek peace with us and trust
that we are given to you
you're given to us

maybe we can be the life bread
to fill the hole
that hope left when it died
stabbed by jagged edges
of promises that broke

maybe we can be the phoenix
risen from the war ashes
to pursue peace
with the passion
of the fury war unleashed

maybe our life can be a sacrament
love's presence in a world that's bent
the first foothold
on the way to hope

january 20, 1973

Contents

These events would have been told in an earlier book had it not been for an extraordinary phone call I received one Sunday last year.

It was about fifteen minutes before church was out and I was at home, an uncommon fact considering who I am and what day it was. I was alone and in a considerable quandary about *Gathered for Power,* which was then less than half written. The publisher's deadline for the manuscript was only five weeks away, and though they insisted the book be short, it was to provide more than casual insight into the charismatic beginnings of my church's renewal. Of course, part of my anxiety was that I had never written a book before, but on that Sunday I was close to tossing in the sponge because I was confused, not because I was a novice.

I had spent the previous night foolishly without sleep, wearying myself into confusion on the horns of a real dilemma. There were two important strands of development that had to be unfolded in the story of renewal, and both of them issued from my acceptance of the rector's post in a dying church located at the edge of Houston's changing inner city. I had to begin from the piece of common history and show what happened both to the church and in the neighborhood. That seemed simple enough. But my sleepless night had been caused by indecision about which way to go first, and the more I pondered the situation the more complicated it appeared. Then I reached an impasse.

A review of the dead-end struggle would go something like

this. I was painfully disillusioned when faced with my church's blindness during several years of pious indifference to squalor at its doorstep. Then because of my desire for a neighborhood type of church, Redeemer Parish failed in the first year of my leadership and I felt much as though I had been suffering through the terminal stages of a beloved friend's disease; I was drained and dispirited. There was afterward a profound grief during the Lenten season of 1964. Out of its depths emerged a new and unexpected vision of the parish church: a corporate community of "brothers," all of them lovers and servants—of Jesus in one another—men, women and children committed primarily to a life of ministry. That vision has been told in *Gathered for Power*.

At the same time I developed a tender yearning for my neighbors. Having begun by believing that insight into a neighborhood's need would be incentive enough to stimulate parochial health, I soon learned that for Redeemer Church that was a false premise, and eventually I despaired over the issue of a gathered church face to face with the world at hand. Of all the parish membership, only I sounded the depths of surrounding need (how like the self-pitying of lonely Elijah that must sound!), and out of the Lenten sorrow that spawned a communitarian hope for my parish church came also a new definition of my ministry—that of an intercessor. I became so identified with the neighborhood as to be baptized in its bondage and pain. Yet I knew the force of God's grace for deliverance; my neighbors did not. Boldly I required of God that He set them free or let me perish because of them, and I refused to relent.

After a year, there came a providential visit to Dave Wilkerson in New York—a marvelous baptism with power— and signs and wonders. Miracles hounded my footsteps; prayers I had been moaning for months began to be answered and people were actually being set free. But that was not all. Scores of well-meaning Christians gathered about Redeemer Church to celebrate this good time of God's favor, and I saw in their midst a possible source of renewal.

It was not to be that simple, however. It had taken miracles to draw the strange assemblage; even stronger stuff would be required to make them stay. At the time, most of them were infatuated with manifestations of power. They sought an easy power . . . miracles of magic . . . a sort of fairy godfather life of Mr. Fixit muddling among the needy. But the spectacle they were watching in Eastwood was heaven's answer to a suffering identified with my intercessions. There was nothing easy about those miracles: they were costly—bought at the price of everything I valued in life.

At first it seemed that Redeemer Church would find new blood from this ad hoc gathering of miracle watchers; that did in fact happen—but not in the way it first seemed. I was joined by only a few of them (my wife, twelve other adults and our children; thirty-three in all) whose lives were prepared and whose hearts were opened to receive power for miracle on the ground of compassion. The twenty-seven (Betty and I then had four children) moved close to the church and now they were my neighbors too. Sensing that sacrifice was the crux of things we laid down our lives in love—for each other and for those whom God sent our way. A charismatic community gathered, but it was not yet in the church. It was just on the fringe.

So the two strands of the story intertwined. The vision of parish renewal and the hope of intercessory power merged, and in time a suffering servant community of charismatics became the renewed parish of Redeemer Church.

On that Sunday last year, I had finished *Gathered for Power* up to my baptism with the Spirit. The story could then have continued along one of two courses. Public miracles attending my ministry after I had returned from New York were the key to understanding why so many people rushed to the parish in late 1964. Reporting those miracles would have been a book in itself. When the crowd scattered in 1965, a few remained to join me in ministry and form the nucleus of a community that would eventually renew the parish. The kind of people these were and the marks of their community life would have been yet another book. Preferring to begin with the first, the story of miracles, I was stymied because my memory failed to come up with some essential facts of the first public wonder.

During a Sunday morning eucharist shortly after my return from New York, a woman had been healed and had left her crutches at the communion rail, but both her name and the extent of her ailment escaped me. The incident was the first public demonstration of a new ministry since I had received the baptism with the Spirit. However, that was seven years earlier—at a time when hundreds of people were coming and going in the first flush of a new enthusiasm—and the woman remained as much a stranger to me afterwards as she had been before. I had no means of finding her. The way her healing had happened, at communion time and without self-consciousness, had given authentication in the eyes of a sophisticated congregation to my baptism with the Spirit. But the event was meaningless without a name and a description of her illness. As far as I could judge, the omission of this pivotal miracle would seriously weaken the story of my early ministry and its effect on the charismatic community that developed out of it. But I was helpless. I had racked my brain trying to remember that event, but finally gave in and thought about finishing *Gathered for Power* without it.

Being very discouraged, I stayed home from church to rest. Then the phone rang.

A pleasant feminine voice asked if she might speak to me. I identified myself and she said, "You probably don't remember me, Brother Pulkingham, but I was healed at your altar rail seven years ago. My name's Margaret Whyte."

I was breathless. "Perhaps I do remember you, Margaret, but I've forgotten what your healing was all about."

"Oh, I had a broken foot," she said off-handedly. "Several bones were fractured, and when I came to the communion rail you prayed for me. I was healed instantly—right in front of everyone—never had any trouble after that. But that's not why I called. I have a friend with so many medical needs you'd never believe it was possible. She needs the Lord, of course, more than anything else, if you know what I mean ...." She hesitated, then continued in a confidential tone. "Her doctors don't *really* try to keep up with the physical things, to say nothing of the spiritual ones. It's hard in a public hospital, isn't it? Anyway, I was praying about her this morning and the Lord nudged me to call you and ask if there's still a spirit-filled doctor in your congregation. My friend's on welfare," she said apologetically. "There can't be a fee. Can you help me with her?"

I gave her a doctor's name and breathed fervent thanksgivings after replacing the telephone receiver. Seven years of silence, broken at the very moment it was most needed. Incredible!

So *Gathered for Power* became the account of my personal Pentecost and of several miraculous events in my ministry that came fast upon it; included is the story of Margaret Whyte's healing. Hundreds gathered in Houston's East End to watch these events; only thirty-three caught a vision of the source of power and stayed to share it. They left their homes, their possessions, their jobs—some left their suffering and despair—because a loving voice had whispered, "Come, follow Me."

They Left Their Nets tells the story of some of the thirty-three and of others who came later to join them. It tells of the formation of a small community, which in three years grew to such a size that by its gentle takeover an Episcopal parish ended one era of life and entered another. Then the parish became the community—a charismatic servant community whose influence now extends around the world.

the
vision

The institutional light of Redeemer Episcopal Church flickered during a change of administration in 1963 and died the following year. I helped lay the struggling parish to rest by intentionally disregarding the expectation of those in the scattered flock who wanted a discreet family chaplain instead of a pastor. Most of them had moved to another section of town anyway; their commitment to the aged and dwindling congregation, made tenuous first by distance, was in a state of serious disaffection toward my new administration. The result was a natural slough, long overdue, which had been averted for years by my predecessor. As one member after another escaped to a better neighborhood, he had secured their allegiance by drawing them into a sizable personal following, but for the most part their loyalty was to him alone. So during the first ten months of my tenure as rector of Redeemer Church, able leadership from lay people dissolved into a pitiful sediment; structural weaknesses appeared in every facet of the parish's life.

The wonder is that I stayed. Eastwood was the worst place to raise a family—inferior schools, no playgrounds, playmates that middle-income Americans would not ordinarily choose for their offspring. But I did stay; and reflection from a distance of nine years provides not the slightest rational clue to my reasons. My life and ministry began looking up later, after I had received a baptism of spiritual power; there were then obvious reasons for remaining in the parish to see the thing through. But the previous ten months had been in every respect the most difficult I had known, and good sense alone would have dictated removal to a more favorable ground.

3

Quite simply, the reasons that compelled me to remain at the parish during those hideous ten months were suprarational—reasons "beyond" the rational. It remains a mystery *why* suprarational factors weighed so heavily in my decision to accept Redeemer Church's call. Such had never happened before; had it not happened then, I might never have gone to the Houston parish—and certainly I would not have stayed the first ten months.

Although the present writing is a sequel to *Gathered for Power*, this story begins a little before the other. It begins eight months before Redeemer Church called me, when I visited the Houston office of the Rev. Scott Field Bailey, who was advisor to the Bishop, John E. Hines. Having just finished a three-year stint as assistant to the rector at St. David's, Austin, I was growing anxious for a rectorship of my own; it was expedient to make the bishop aware of my desire. The Houston visit was as much personal as it was business though, because Scott and I had been friends for the twelve years since my reception into the Episcopal Church under his pastorate at All Saints' in Austin. When he reported that there were no foreseeable openings among diocesan parishes of a size to interest me, two old friends fell to chit-chat.

"Graham, did you hear what happened to Bob Kemp?" he queried casually about a seminary classmate.

"No," I said with anticipation. Scott was not given to gossip, and his question carried a tinge of foreboding. "What happened to him?"

"He was fired."

"What do you mean, 'fired'?" I asked intently. "You mean by a church?"

"Not the church—its rector. Dr. Harris just up and fired him one day last week."

I realized that Bob's whereabouts since we graduated six years earlier were a mystery to me. I had never heard of Dr. Harris.

"I guess I don't know where he's been lately," I admitted hesitantly.

4

"Right here in Houston. Graham, you mean you don't keep up with the alumni? Shame," he chided with kindly laughter. "If you're not careful you'll end up a loner. Bob's been an assistant at Redeemer Church in the East End for a couple of years now. I don't know much about the parish or old Dr. Harris either, but he's been rector there for a long time."

Scott was crouched forward in a low chair studying the rug at his feet. With one heavy eyebrow cocked he glanced up at me and asked, "Ever been out there?"

I shook my head, puzzled.

"It's a run-down neighborhood," he said frowning. "Shabby. I don't know how the parish makes it, to tell the truth. But poor old Bob, they gave him a pay check the other day and told him to move out . . . just like that . . . skedaddle! It's a pity too. He's got a big family, and we've nothing to offer him right now."

How could I have been in the Diocese of Texas for thirteen years, I wondered, and never have heard of Dr. Harris or Redeemer Church?

"Scott," I said incredulously, "why have I never heard of the place?"

"Oh," he hesitated, "Dr. Harris is a bit of an isolationist, Graham." Then he added uncritically, "You know—an old timer—doesn't understand the bishop's leadership. John's been working with the situation so I don't know much about it personally. But keep Bob in your prayers, will you? He'll need something in a hurry."

My curiosity was challenged. Before starting westward toward Austin I drove southeast from downtown Houston to the neighborhood of Redeemer Parish. There on the edge of a tiny pocket of neat, well-worn houses—in glaring contrast to their surroundings—was a triangular block of massive grey buildings topped with bright red Spanish-tile roofing. It was the church property. The day was wintry, raining, cold and unfriendly; and the parish buildings seemed like an enormous intrusion into the otherwise dishevelled and slovenly milieu. Standing idly at an uncurtained window in one of the grey

5

buildings was an elderly man in clerical collar. *That must be Dr. Harris,* I thought, driving slowly by. Then another thought came fast upon that one; it was matter-of-fact but occurred with such force that a chill ran the length of my spine. *Before long you'll be standing at that window in his place, Graham.*

Hmm, I mused distractedly. *Where in the world did that come from? Didn't think I was so pressed to make a change.*

Out of curiosity—or was it "just in case"?—I looked again at the monstrous edifices covering a full city block and noticed that the buildings looked impressive. Something in my self-importance was satisfied by the observation. Then giving the neighborhood a better scrutiny I tasted its degradation for the first time.

Several months passed. Then one day I received a phone call from the senior warden of Houston's Church of the Redeemer and my heart leaped suddenly, pounding with such force that I feared the din would be heard at the other end. The caller's name was Bob Evans. He told me that Dr. Harris, recently afflicted by a series of heart attacks, had been advised to retire, and the parish was in search of a new rector. The names of forty priests, mine among them, had been gathered from various sources by a committee of the vestry; each man was being approached by telephone to check on his availability. A letter to be sent later would officially open conversation and briefly state the job description. Several visits should be expected from teams of vestrymen until the number of eligible candidates was reduced to three, who in turn would be invited to take a Sunday of services in the parish. Finally a selection would be made and a man called.

A few weeks later I was named among the three. My turn for a Sunday of ministry came and went smoothly, except for personal disappointment in the music at the eucharist. At the close of the service a woman approached me and said, "The Holy Spirit has told me you will be our new rector." I was offended—perhaps because she claimed it to be a statement made by the Spirit rather than an idea of her own—but

6

in any case I replied, with inexcusable rudeness, "Well, I hope He has the decency to tell me about it." She replied graciously and withdrew.

The woman was Grace Murray, who had been a member of Redeemer Church for decades. During the eight years preceding my rectorship she had been openly ridiculed and at times persecuted for her involvement with pentecostalists. After five years of unremitting harassment she had been tempted to leave her home church and join a small independent group of friends, but they counseled her to remain where she was. It seems they had faith that God would give to Redeemer Church a man walking in the Spirit. She had believed with them, and at our first meeting saw that man in me. In spite of my rudeness her faithful eyes continued the vision until it came to pass fifteen months later. Grace's prayers and tears, perhaps more than anything else, brought down heaven's renewing life for her home church.

So I was called to be the new rector of a dying parish in Houston's unsettled East End. The process was similar to the way any rector might be selected and called to a troubled Episcopal church: a vestry's analysis, its often factious deliberations and the deft political leadership of some—all played their part. So did the opinions of influential members and a propitious word here and there from the bishop. But there was another, an unfamiliar element in this call. I have termed it "suprarational" rather than "supernatural" in order to distinguish it from the spiritual factor in every call to Christian leadership. As I saw it at the time, a special miracle was underway, and I was convinced that God had put me in Redeemer Parish for some unique purpose. It seemed inappropriate to speak to anyone of my unusual first encounter with the church and its neighborhood. In spite of this timidity, however, I accepted the call to Houston with eager anticipation of awesome and wonderful things waiting just around the corner.

Chapter II

So Moses returned to the Lord and said, "Alas; this people have sinned a great sin; they have made for themselves gods of gold. But now, if thou wilt forgive their sin—and if not, blot me, I pray thee, out of thy book which thou hast written." But the Lord said to Moses, "Whoever has sinned against me, him will I blot out of my book. But now go, lead the people to the place of which I have spoken to you; behold my angel shall go before you. . . ."

Ex. 32:31-34

The folk of Eastwood were not entirely unfamiliar to me when in the winter of 1963 I furrowed deep into their lives. A few months earlier, after nights had already grown colder than naked arms could bear, the warmth of our parish hall gym was opened to a sizable group of their youngsters who habitually roamed the neighborhood until the early morning hours. Though personally distant, they responded to the offer by the score. From the looks of things nobody cared for them much—how they were dressed, where they went, who they were with. But my own insights into their upbringing became sensitive during several weeks of close nightly observation. They were street urchins, dragged into maturity by the time they were sixteen and filled with fears because they had been fending for themselves in a hostile world from the time they were twelve.

Occasionally in the wake of one of these disordered lives I encountered a parent (rarely two). They were suspicious and fearful, and they lumped me together with other public officials who made regular intrusions into their lives. I looked and acted like a helper, though I was not from the schools, welfare department or juvenile courts.

Church was among the least of their interests; I doubt they had ever even conversed with "the preacher." I and my religion were largely the object of their indifference, not as a matter of personal affront, but simply because nothing in the nature of their relationship to public officials was personal. They had no personal way of dealing with a man while anticipating what might be extracted from him. However, familiarity eventually proved me to be empty handed. I was useless, or at best redundant, and public official with little to give, no tangible offering. My prayers were fruitless, and my irrelevant message was contemptible in their ears because it sounded like the inveiglements of so many itinerant preachers who were as likely to milk widows of a mite as they were to speak words of salvation.

Soon their reticence in our relationship ceased, and I noticed complaint on the edge of every voice. They were suddenly more talkative but it felt strangely as though their words were waging a useless campaign for my support against something unknown to me and as yet unnamed by them. Then came their angry revenge—not against me for still there was nothing personal in our relationship, but against the parish and its smug security. In a state of shock I watched the church property—and its rector—become scapegoats in the pitiless hands of a nightly rabble. With impunity these poor took access to our middle-class lives because we had welcomed them there. From that vantage point the more aggressive among them gained first-hand intercourse with an institution of the rich and a vulgar root of bitterness was laid bare. Their violence was aimed really at an affluent society, but Redeemer Church was at the brunt of it, and we were defenseless.

By then it was late spring and the parish was already on its last leg; like a stricken bird fluttering at a cat's play, its good works were spent in wasted efforts. The doors to the gym were padlocked again, and the onslaught ceased.

9

I was in despair. Everything that was offered had been despised, and finally the church withdrew.

But how could I retreat? My soul was stuck fast in extraordinary compassion for the neighborhood and its struggling folk. Perhaps the church had failed to call forth the kingdom of God's love, but during the past several months something in me had been irreversibly altered and I refused to back off. Instead the tattered self-image of trained religious officialdom went by the board and simply as a fellow human I carried my fervent concern out among the people—on the streets, in their apartments, at the curbsides by night. Also I took the burden of it into a lonely basement chapel which for six weeks, from Ash Wednesday to Easter, became my tomb of despair.

It was in that lonely chapel during Lent that I became a visionary. The revelations I received were not flights of fancy or mere daydreams, nor were they conclusions drawn from rapidly reasoned processes. They were like the vision seen by Peter in a noonday trance on the rooftop when the Lord prepared him to unlock the kingdom's gates for a God-fearing Gentile named Cornelius. In the unveiling of two stark future moments I visualized the church in Eastwood as it was to be—a loving, sharing, serving community of praise and thanksgiving, and I saw the ministry, or more particularly I saw my own ministry as it was to be—charismatic.

Out of my lonely suffering was emerging a new hope, not a new self-image: the possibility of authority I had never before dreamed available to the sons of men, but I wanted it. It was not ecclesial authority; it was authority given directly by the author of life Himself, an authenticating power to overcome opposing works of darkness and stop their destruction at the wellspring or subdue them at the flood. It involved a mysterious endowment of power to impart life for death, health for sickness, and freedom for bondage.

I had never given much thought to the term "intercessor" or to the sort of preparation and experience such a ministry entailed. The word had to my mind described an office fulfilled chiefly, or perhaps solely, in the ministry of Christ Himself. In practice, therefore, I imagined intercessions to be vicarious, amounting on my part to little more than desiring good for others in the midst of their ill—and saying so in quiet meditation or in formal utterances of prayer. What supplications I made for the neighborhood folk began in that way: honest intercessory prayers for the poor, the sick and those who were bound. But as I walked deeper into the fiber of their humanity my own soul turned sick, until eventually I shared with them a common pain of anguish. No longer were there thoughts of praying for the "poor"; I prayed for us, and my intercessions involved a far more fervent pleading.

In the gloom of my basement retreat, teetering at the brink of hopelessness concerning any kind of viable ministry to the poor, I clung helplessly to a thin comfort. God—if He would—could surely do something to relieve such a frightful state as theirs was. Often I had a gnawing uncertainty, however. *Why had He not already done so?* While I hung on that edge of disillusionment, some engaging thoughts met me in my meditations.

Stop asking God to do what you want done. Do it yourself.

But, I argued, *I've done all I can, and nothing works. Besides, it's a matter of changing lives, not just helping folk.*

Right, was the rejoinder, *you were sent to change people's lives. There are many faultfinders, and hordes to pity the poor, but your prayers will move me toward them as you open your own life and make yourself vulnerable to their despair. That's how my love draws close to them; it happens in you. When your souls have come close enough to touch each other, reach out and give them my life. But remember, when you offer my life to someone else, make available to him everything I've given you. Everything—have you thought? I'll not hear your prayers for a hungry man if you won't feed him. Nor will I heed your pleas for a lonely man*

11

or a man trapped in poverty unless you're willing to take him into the bosom of your own family and pay his debts out of your own purse.

Astonishing! I had always thought it presumptuous to be definite concerning God's will in a given matter, but to go beyond that and ask for the ability to do for others no less than what He would do if He were right here!

These were troublesome thoughts about ministry. How often I had been counseled not to become personally involved. Here was a concept of involvement requiring total commitment to those being served: a living sacrifice—my life for theirs.

The dialogue continued.

Why should that surprise you? You've been sent in my name, with my authority.

Yes, I retorted, *but not to take your place.*

In a sense you have been sent to take my place. You must love with my love, suffer with my suffering, forgive with my forgiveness in the places where I send you; and I'll enable you then to pray effectually with my faith and to do miracles with my power. You've seen the needy lives around you: diseased, bound, suffering and tormented by sin; you've asked me to open their blind eyes and deaf ears, and to soften their hardened hearts. I'll do it, all of it—at your hands. I'm offering you grace enough for that. But grace of this kind is costly, not free like the grace I give for yourself. It's free for them, but if you continue to serve me in the needs of these people, in one way or another I'll require your life at their hands.

How can these things be? My heart pleaded with earnestness.

By my Spirit.

Until then the biblical phrase "by my Spirit" was a familiar prophetic dictum. It had religious meanings but they were far too distant from where life was really lived. Slowly the impact of its truth began filtering into my world of common thought and parlance. There it produced an insatiable hunger for immersion in the power the words promised.

I had gone to Redeemer Church as an average Episcopal minister of the gospel. I leaned moderately then in the direction of liberal theology and had an active social conscience. Had someone asked, I might glibly have defined my function as an ordained minister. Now I would hesitate, and my concepts would be expressed in fewer task-oriented terms than they were then. But I was an honest man, well trained, and a willing ecclesiastical servant who was committed (within civilized limits of self-sacrifice) to the furtherance of Christ's gospel. In the best sense of the words, I was a "paid professional."

However, when confronted with the entirely unfamiliar context of this parish, my first professional instinct was caution. Little by little, having scouted out the land, I became involved—first of all on my terms—until I had gone beyond the place of no return. Then I was fully involved—on compassion's terms. Not until then was I of much use in the vision God had been shaping for the future of Redeemer Church.

By Easter 1964 the facts of my ministry had changed so radically as to make it almost unrecognizable. I no longer valued myself as an official of any kind, and the fine professional training I had received had served only to confuse at a critical juncture. However, a new and nonofficial description of ministry was crystallizing. It centered around a life of intercessory power in prayer.

I asked myself a momentous question: *Where now for me are God's people to be found? In a cold, professional Sunday liturgy or in that Eastwood whirligig of sin?*

And where now was my help to be found? Every pretentiousness of place and position had vanished; the church had failed and so had I. Accepting the failure of both as a mysterious but praiseworthy gift, I abandoned myself to the God of inscrutable callings. I realized, perhaps for the first time, that my hope lay simply in him.

Baptized in love's suffering and crippled by my neighbors' infirmities, I cried out for our miserable flesh, not theirs only but mine also, because it was impossible to disentangle our

13

lives. They continued their crying too—whimpering in angry despair. But somehow I worked through anger and despair into a position of faith and commended myself to God on their behalf.

One thing more was necessary. In the fellowship of their suffering I would prove the sufficiency of Christ's grace and commend myself to them on His behalf.

Chapter III

Moses said to the Lord, "See, thou sayest to me, 'Bring up this people'; but thou hast not let me know whom thou wilt send with me. Yet thou hast said, 'I know you by name, and you have also found favor in my sight.' Now therefore, I pray thee, if I have found favor in thy sight, show me now thy ways, that I may know thee and find favor in thy sight. . . ." And he said, "My presence will go with you, and I will give you rest."

Ex. 33:12-14

I had only heard of *The Cross and the Switchblade,* but its author's fame reached my ears and from the sound of things Dave Wilkerson was familiar with the fellowship of Christ's sufferings. We met in August 1964 at his Brooklyn headquarters, in an encounter that was one of three crucial stages in shaping the future of my ministry. He prayed for me. In my eyes his credibility before God was not to be impeached, and when he prayed a spiritual baptism descended without fanfare and infused my life with long-awaited powers.

It was not simply a matter of ecstasy during his prayer that caused me to claim a special work of grace over and above salvation, a "baptism with the Spirit." The several months of baptism with suffering that finally led me into the New York experience, and the astonishing months of baptism with power following it, were far more cogent in commending Jesus' own baptism than was ecstasy. In fact, the gospel record seems not to emphasize ecstasy as an intrinsic mark of Jesus' ministry; and it was that very thing—His ministry, or the empowering source of it—I was in search of when everything else failed in Houston. Two of my life's deepest and strongest spiritual moments, the Eastwood suffering of compassion and the ensuing powers of intercession, were not mystical ecstacies in any commonly accepted sense; they were the most concrete yet utterly godly thrusts into the horizontal plane that I had known until then. There was nothing hidden or private about either of them and I met Christ face to face in both. Ecstasy, on the other hand, was a private matter. It happened in the vertical plane of mystical rapture, and involved an intensive moment of fellowship with God while I was singularly overwhelmed by His favor and love.

Suffering, ecstasy, power. They all happened to me dramatically during 1964, and all of them continue to be an intimate part of my pilgrimage with Jesus. But none of the three is of greater significance than the others, either as a spiritual experience or in describing the pentecostal work of grace that was added to my Christian walk. Therefore when sectarian voices inquire whether I have received the Holy Spirit since I believed (and I am confident they refer to a special unction or endowment of the Spirit beyond initial steps toward salvation), my answer is an unequivocal, "Yes." There is a proviso, however: my baptism with the Spirit occurred over the course of a full year in which not one single moment was more important, or more telling, than another. Will there be other times of such intense personal spiritual awakening? How can I say. I can only state that I doubt there will ever be another year like 1964.

What of the experience of speaking in unknown tongues, and what is its relation to my baptism with the Spirit? I have received that controversial gift and exercise it probably as much as most. It was a parallel but, I must admit, irrelevant phenomenon among the world-shattering events in my personal life during the year of my visit to Dave Wilkerson. That particular charism was experienced much later. The gift of unknown tongues was received in the midst of ministering

16

power, while healings and miracles were already at work. So for the inquirer seeking to understand initial forces for renewal loosed in Redeemer Church I have no easy answer. But I disavow the claim that it all began simply in a private moment of spiritual baptism with the alleged "evidence of speaking in other tongues."

These comments are not an attempt to cast doubt upon ecstatic experience or the gift of unknown tongues. Both can be of God. They are increasingly prevalent in this present age of radical social change and Christian disillusionment. And the record must be kept straight: it was charisms—especially miracles, healings and tongues—that first attracted hundreds of people to my ministry in Redeemer Church. Tales of strange and wonderful things—charismatic things—brought them to my parish neighborhood.

Redeemer Church could never have found renewal as it later developed had not spiritual gifts been foremost in my expectations after returning from New York. I earnestly sought their effect in ministry, even to the point of being willing for pentecostal excesses to be unleashed. Let them run wild if they would. What did it matter? I had resolute faith in the God of my visions, being assured that a loving community could tame even the most ardent enthusiasts and harness them for the work of renewal.

Prophecy engendered faith, and faith brought forth works of power: my expectancy of spiritual gifts was not disappointed. During the fall of 1964 spontaneous utterances of prayer were producing concrete, unambiguous results. How? I am not sure I can say; this was an initiatory period and none of the ministry resulting from charisms was anticipated —it just happened, seemingly without rhyme or reason. The outreach of God's grace, though varied, was discriminating and mysterious. Occasions for prayer might be in a telephone ring, at a door knock or under a nearby bush. For example, someone in the parish might have fallen ill, and there would be a remarkable healing at my touch; or an inveterate tramp

17

lost for years in alcoholism might wander by the rectory and find grace for new life in my exhortations and counsel.

No matter how impossible the need, at the beginning there was an average of "success in prayer"—if I may use so cheeky a phrase—that was better than two out of three, a fact that encouraged me to expect ministering results at the highest level of faith. Each unpredictable day became a fresh new adventure.

I was as surprised as the next fellow at this turn of events—the more so because I saw the frequency and extent of miracle. I saw perfect vision restored to badly impaired eyesight, the near deaf enabled to hear, broken bones and torn flesh undergoing instant and perfect healing, palpable growths and diagnosed cancers vanishing within moments of prayer. There were cures of chronic schizophrenia and severe emotional disturbances; addictive personalities were healed and released; broken relationships were mended; food and other necessaries appeared as from nowhere; household pests vanished at the command of prayer; berserk animals—and sometimes humans—were subdued with a word. And these are only a few of the many incredible things that were going on.

I spent the last quarter of 1964 passing from wonder to wonder in a state of semishock. Between times there were prayer and weeping. Yes, I still wept with compassion; but now there was also joy, and joyful tears of gratitude because I had found grace to commend the Lord of all goodness to some of my neighbors. The vision I had seen of intercessory power was becoming real in my ministry.

Chapter IV

And [Moses] said to [the Lord], "If thy presence will not go with me, do not carry us up from here. For how shall it be known that I have found favor in thy sight, I and thy people? Is it not in thy going with us, so that we are distinct, I and thy people, from all other people that are upon the face of the earth?"

Ex. 33:15,16

The lightning speed of rumors reporting me to be a miracle worker jolted my friends and complicated my life unexpectedly. Within a few weeks after I returned to Houston from New York, people from miles around began calling on me. Sometimes the call was by telephone, perhaps a concerned friend or a curiosity seeker; but if there was a knock at the rectory door usually life became embroiled with yet another stranger bearing outlandish and fascinating tales in explanation of his presence. The attraction was singular: miracles. The callers, however, were an indiscriminate scattering of American society whose interest in me, generally speaking, fell into one of two categories: they were the needy or the helpful.

I was convinced irrevocably that there was only one kind of Christian ministry that could be helpful to the people in Eastwood; it assumed life commitment to them in their suffering condition. Evangelistic zeal, humanitarian pity, infatuation with supernatural signs of mercy were not enough. Those who came to be helpful were committed in life at some other place; they were mobile and could choose the terms and the depth of their ministering involvement by traveling back and forth to the parish neighborhood. But the needy who appeared from elsewhere came by city bus that probably took hours in transit, or they drove from out of town in vehicles too unreliable for commuting. Suddenly the rectory was swamped with them, and although it would be impossible to exaggerate the frantic state this caused in my family's life, it was a necessary step in the direction of intercessory ministry.

A simple condition of need was rarely enough to bring forth miracles in the lives of my neighbors or visitors. Other ingredients had to be mixed in. I observed that those who were favored with obvious demonstrations of power were humble souls with a subtle personal quality of submissiveness. In opening to me their need they found I was a man, complex and intense, offering them a simple and unswerving faith; they yielded and were eager to share not only their needs but the whole of their human condition. That response must surely have been a work of God's sovereign grace wrought in them by the spirit of Christ's compassion. The others who came asking for miracle as though they sought some magical panacea usually returned home untouched—not always unhelped, but untouched in their need.

For me, at least to begin with, the fellowship of Christ's sufferings was a real, intensely personal relationship with certain despised humans. I had gone to the poor as their helper, and though as helpless as they in their grief, and as perplexed, I was not despairing. The grace of God's mercy "reduced" me to being their friend (I would never before have chosen to be the lover of such souls as theirs), and they cast me down in anger and mistrust, but I was not destroyed. In my weakness God delivered me into a kind of death for Jesus' sake and with helpless tears of anguish for these friends I laid my life down, unconditionally. Then came an assurance of unquenchable faith. Soon there were stirrings of life in some of my neighbors—a very few of them. Earlier they had been as calloused and dead to the gospel as the others, but now they approached me with honest offerings of their troubled and sick selves. It was not to a helper that they came now, or to a symbol of impersonal affluence; they came to me as a new friend who spoke words of faith about his merciful and loving Christ. They must have seen the life of Jesus mysteriously alive in the flesh of my humanity, because their approach was on His ground of love and no longer on their ground of suffering. We prayed together. We submitted to each other's words and touch. Then God moved upon our lives with awesome and magnificent strength to impart the seeds of health-giving life in the midst of abominations. Drawn together in this power, we were exhilarated beyond measure and found fresh unbridled communion together in miracles, in new freedom and in the embrace of love's peace.

My family's life was almost a shambles during the last three months of 1964. On some nights there were a dozen or more people curled up asleep in chairs or on pallets; waking hours became an incessant routine of finger food, counsel, and prayer meetings. The church and rectory looked like a refugee camp. But God was not a wholesaler. From among the scores of persons involved during those heady weeks at the beginning only a few handfuls of wonders were seen. In the pressure of it all, though, I learned the subtle distinction between those who would come no closer than was necessary to offer simply their misery, and those unpredictable few who would openly reveal themselves in the context of their need. The latter found miracles and release in fellowship, and they found their own faith too; sometimes it took moments, sometimes hours, days, weeks, months or even years, but it happened. The others went elsewhere with their untouched suffering, or they returned home to a familiar despair.

Unrestricted fellowship was the decisive ingredient for effective ministry in those days, whether for the needy or for the helpful. At the outset there were as many hopeful Christians who appeared with offerings of help as there were desperate souls who sought it. But not many of either found grace or willingness to alter their lives sufficiently to experience ministering power—which was the only effective help I had to offer or to share. Most who came in the first flush of enthusiasm eventually settled back into customary patterns of life in the suburbs they came from.

Not all did, however, and the exceptions were important. Within six weeks after I returned from New York, four families and several single women had been drawn dramatically into my fellowship and ministry. These came with an openness to radical life change and a willingness to stay. The adults, prepared by personal circumstance to make sacrifices, were ready to give themselves unconditionally as instruments of God's ministering Spirit. They discovered charismatic gifts of their own, and their prayers worked wonders. Feeling an undeniable compulsion to lay everything else aside, they involved themselves more and more in the life of the parish neighborhood. Some traveled more than a hundred miles a day, mysteriously drawn by a charisma of love, driven by an unslakable thirst for fellowship with one another.

A community was gathering: a people called forth from despair, like Lazarus called from the tomb by Jesus' loving voice. Our grave clothes unraveled and began slowly falling away; we were being released into the power of pure, fervent love for one another regardless of background and condition of life.

Some of us—the halt and the hale—met daily for prayer, encouragement in the scriptures, and fellowship. When in early 1965 the uncontrollable number of visitors diminished abruptly, community membership began to be defined. It was an easy definition: we were unable to stay away from each other. An occasional visitor still straggled in, and some folk went away, but for the most part our lives had returned to anonymity and they were so intertwined that it was difficult to be separated even for a few hours of work or sleep. A middle-aged mother said to me through her beaming smile one day, "If I loved you any better, brother, we'd be sinnin' together." Her child's broken leg had recently been healed while we were praying for her.

22

Then the pressures of our community life began to be felt. Some of us met to encourage one another in prayer and to search the scriptures twice daily. In addition, all day Saturday was spent in fellowship and sharing at one community home or another, and two nights a week were set aside for public meetings, which at once drew a sympathetic following. Community membership increased, slowly but persistently; the challenge to keep faith and love alive increased a hundredfold. Demands for pastoral leadership and community-oriented teaching fell heavily on a few of the more stable members of the community; that was a new experience for all of us and the emerging leadership had to be nimble and quick to stay one step ahead of the others. From the earliest stages in our development these "overseers" (I was among them, though not in charge) assumed the task of shaping, directing and ordering the community's life. Our responsibilities forced us together more often than the rest and we experienced astonishing depths of fellowship; powerful spiritual gifts for building a community began to emerge.

On Easter Monday morning in 1965 the ministering community of intercessors took a more formal look at itself. Five of us gathered to discuss the matter. We continued daily at 5:30 a.m., about an hour before the general morning prayer time, having decided to pray and listen carefully for what the Lord was saying about the future of our life together. Others joined us and soon there was about a dozen, all willing to share their lives with one another as a means of fostering stable community life. This was a willingness reflecting major commitments to ministry, because every resource we could command was being called upon to meet the growing community's needs.

In a matter of weeks it was clear what the Lord was saying. One morning we put our lives on the altar and gave them to the Christ of compassion, saying in effect, "Brother, my life is in your hands; all I have, spiritual and otherwise, is yours. Let's share our resourcefulness together freely and make of it a common, single life available to whomever the

23

Lord sends us to love and serve." Although those exact words were not spoken, that was the spirit of our commitment. As a final act of faith our possessions, our earnings and savings, our bank books and insurance policies were given to the Lord by making them available to each other. That was for me a moment of breathtaking earnestness: trusting my life to the Lord in my brothers. It was an informal agreement. Nothing changed hands at the moment and each continued to administer his own affairs, but from that time forward no one regarded the things he possessed as his own.

A charismatic community of intercession had formed, and a vital issue was raised. Each in the privacy of his own mind wondered whether in the entirety of our lives we were prepared to move into the parish neighborhood and live there with the poor. We knew that our community life would involve immediately some of the neediest folk we had met; God was already moving miraculously in several of their lives and they were pressing up close in genuine warmth of fellowship. But there was no cause to worry; in the context of faith it seemed a simple matter to share the poverty of others. We were a community and everything belonged to Jesus; in Him we trusted in our love for each other and refused to believe He was unable somehow to work a perfection of peace among us. That morning the air sparkled with an electrifying sense that for some sovereign purpose of God we were being gathered into a tiny fold tucked away in the covert of his tenderest care.

By the following August the foundation was completed: everyone had moved into Eastwood neighborhood and the community defined its core to be six households huddled in the shadow of Redeemer Church. Among the members were a doctor, a lawyer, a preacher, a laborer, an engineer, several teachers, an editor and a librarian as well as housewives, school children and babies. There were also some "indigenous" poor and some who had moved into the neighborhood from elsewhere, taking up residence in nearby apartments or

24

small houses. There were some very disturbed souls. These, we moved into the six core households for intensive ministry.

Community leaders—the doctor, lawyer, preacher, laborer, engineer and some of the women—met daily. The whole community, numbering about a hundred souls, met twice a week at the Tuesday and Friday night meetings. Sunday morning saw most of us, but not all, at Redeemer's Sunday Eucharist. At an informal level there was daily intermingling in Bible sharing, fellowship and prayer.

It was not a "church" community established by a bishop, vestry or ordained minister. It was a community called forth by prophetic visions and established by the authority of our radical commitment to one another in love; we found no occasion or need for a covenant agreement or for a charter or for rules. The authority of our life together—love—was the rule by which we lived; love of the brethren belonged more and more to our peace.

For the most part people were afraid of us in those beginning days. We spoke faith, which was attractive, and the wonders faith performed were laudable. But our life style looked onerous to all but those who by choice or circumstance had been made poor and selfless.

One might say that as the world judges, we had "gone for broke."

the
community

Chapter V

Not a church, though perhaps more broadly ecclesial than vast numbers of Episcopal parishes; not a family or clan, though bound together by spiritual cords far stronger than the ties of blood kinship; not a welfare organization, though in many instances more successful in dealing with the poor than all the helping professions put together; not a religious order, though perhaps more devout and disciplined in praise than the average cloister; a charismatic community of witnesses to the death and resurrection of God's compassion in Jesus had been formed in Houston's East End out of a fistful of urban Americana.

Who were they, like Gideons clambering from behind the winepresses of despair and disillusionment to war against Midianite forces in the American social order? Did they think they were wise—threatening the social structure in such an easy manner? Surely only fools and ne'er-do-wells would leave their nets to follow so whimsical a sound of sharing and call it the voice of Jesus.

Perhaps. But let them speak for themselves. Here is a sampling of the earliest community membership. I will personally introduce one young man and a family of six; the rest will introduce themselves, in their own words where available. For reasons that are obvious, several of the persons appear under a pseudonym.

There was Tony, sloe-eyed and sallow, an intellectual with middle-class background whose graduate degree in languages had led him to lonely isolation somewhere in France. He was unemployed. In France, a "voice" called him to the pious rigors of a wandering hermit and he obeyed, one scant meal and four hours sleep daily serving as appropriate monkish fare. Apparently Tony's sensitive soul had lost touch with the realities of his life while he was in France. His wife of college days stayed behind in America to finish a doctoral degree and became estranged from him during this European absence. They were later divorced.

He spent several weeks roving through the Western world in search of universal religious truths, and while in Egypt happened upon a bona fide mummy, available for purchase. It became a cohort of his meditations and a boon companion to his wanderings from one end of Europe to the other, until customs regulations forced him to abandon it before reentry into the United States. He arrived home in a state of complete collapse. Several weeks in a Houston mental hospital restored him to a semblance of health and he was released. But the frugal practices and the monkish self-image were tenaciously held, and they were undoubtedly intensified by association with the undisciplined members of a zealous prayer group on the fringe of an Episcopal congregation near his home.

Tony was a very sick man, schizophrenic with a bizarre sort of religious veneer. He underwent several hospitalizations, but nothing could shatter his fixation about personal religious asceticism, and before long he began to look the part of a Rasputin—wild-eyed and scraggy.

One morning I was confronted at my office door by a hollow-cheeked, tonsured young man who said nothing at all but returned my smile with an angry stare. Tony refused to enter the office but in two curt phrases dispatched his business.

"You have the Spirit?"

I nodded, "Yes," cautiously.

"Here's some of my poetry. Maybe you'll find time to read it." He turned and vanished down the steps into the street.

That was our first encounter.

Glancing at a few of the tightly intellectual, sinuous and flowery lines filled with obscure religious symbols, I threw the papers away and forgot the incident until several weeks later.

One Sunday during the sermon at Eucharist Tony skulked into the corner of a back pew and remained huddled there in the shadows. When the congregation had thinned I heard a knock at the vestry door; it was Tony, confused and scattered, weighing considerably more than when I last saw him. He had just been released from the hospital again. On the Sunday following his visit to my office he had entered a church and for some vague purpose of protest stood barefoot and immovable at the altar rail during the main morning service; clad in dirty dungarees, with his shirt worn back to front, his unkempt presence an embarrassment to the congregation. The next day he had been committed to a hospital for safekeeping.

As I removed my vestments we talked—or rather I talked while Tony nodded in answer to my questions; otherwise he stared. The fiery anger earlier so obvious in his jet black eyes was now gone, and though his features were soft he looked defeated. I asked if I might help.

"I don't know," he said in confusion. "I'll go back to washing dishes tomorrow. They kept my job for me. But I can stay with my mother till I get a room."

"Tony," I volunteered, "there's a small group of us that prays together every morning at 5:30. Would it help if you joined us?"

He smiled. Then I saw his stomach muscles jump in a strange little tic and his shoulder twitched oddly as he answered, "Yes, I suppose. If I can make it."

"What's the matter? Don't you have a car?"

"Yes, but it's a rattletrap. It keeps stalling—especially in the morning when it's cold."

"Maybe someone could come and get you."

"Oh no," he said quickly. "No, I'll try it. Five-thirty, eh? Where?"

"In the chapel down there." I pointed to a stairwell outside the vestry door.

"OK, I'll try and make it. See you then." He hesitated at the door before closing it. "I won't be in your way, will I?"

"No, of course not," I reassured him. "We'll be glad to have you."

He left. The next morning Tony was in the chapel before anyone else. He sat quietly with his head bowed on his chest in a shadowy corner of the room. Our morning prayer time was always quite informal; there was no visible leadership or customary order. Only a dozen or fifteen of us attended and when anyone wanted to volunteer a prayer or a chorus or read from the Bible he was free to do so. That morning I sat in a pew next to Tony. At times during the quiet prayers and singing a twitching of his body could be felt jostling our pew. I remarked to myself how strange it seemed. Was Tony a spastic?

He was there again the next morning and when told of the Tuesday and Friday night larger meetings he promised to come. The meetings on Tuesday night generally had an attendance of about a hundred persons, meeting informally in a large classroom. Tony arrived late and took a chair by the door at the very back, a fact for which I was soon grateful. We were on our feet singing a hymn of praise as he entered. When he was settled—and staring at a hymnal though not singing from it—I saw slight evidence of a twitch in his body. By the time the last stanza was well underway he had given two sideways lurches as though catching himself before falling. His eyes were closed, his face looked tight and every muscle in his body was straining. The singing stopped and we sat down. During the service he sat quietly, head bowed and hands folded over crossed knees. Customarily, we stood for a closing hymn. That night it was glorious, "Crown Him with Many Crowns" to the tune *Diademata*. But during the crescendo of our praises I heard a chilling noise overpowering the piano and voices. Looking at its source I was aghast to see Tony, twisting and convulsed, growling through his lips sounds that would surely have been roared were his teeth not clenched. Our spirits were dampened as one after another of the worshipers heard his strange noises, responded with alarm and stopped singing; the last stanza was almost a piano solo.

Afterward I went to Tony, my face showing obvious concern, I am sure. He was painfully ashamed and apologized; a little of the earlier anger flashed in his eyes.

"You see," he explained, "this happens sometimes when I'm with people who get excited about God. It spoils my detachment." He gave a slight twitch. "You know, you have to be detached to meditate properly."

I had no idea what he was talking about—detachment. It sounded like the teaching of the German mystic, Meister Eckhardt, whose ascetical theories I scanned in seminary.

"Tony, when did this begin?"

"When I was baptized with the Spirit last year," he said, closing his eyes and tightening his lips. "It began after I went home from the meeting and tongues came to me." His last few words were forced through clenched teeth, and as soon as the sentence was finished he lisped nonsense sounds through a leering mouth. Then the jerking began. He continued, eyes closed, speaking what I assumed was his version of the "gift" of tongues and his convulsions once again became violent. My response was amazement and outright alarm. Unable to watch the spectacle I literally shouted, "Tony, *stop* that!" He gave a start, opened his eyes and looked at me, then hung his head in shame. The trance was over. I was suddenly overwhelmed by a great sympathy for the pathetic and lonely figure standing in front of me; reaching out I took him in my arms. He yielded to my embrace for a moment, then stiffened and backed away. "Thanks," he murmured, "I'm OK now." I decided to pursue the matter at another time.

Tony became a regular attendant at community meetings. It was commonplace for him to be heard growling or seen convulsing during hymns and prayers of praise. Often simple ejaculations such as "Praise the Lord" or "Hallelujah" caused a twitch. We quickly learned that a mature person without fear of Tony's behavior, one who would speak with authority to him, could easily dispel the trances by a whispered command. But our attempts at prayer with laying on of hands to rid him of the plaguing thing brought only hideous spasms in his body; once during our prayers Tony flipped from a standing position and flew head over heels, landing two pews away on his back.

We loved Tony. Some of us fasted and prayed especially for his deliverance. Then one day it occurred to me that he was possessed with a religious spirit—an exhibitionist spirit of "divination" like the one described in Acts 16 where Paul is at prayer with his converts. I told Tony these thoughts, and we decided to continue secretly in prayer for his deliverance but ignore the disturbing behavior. Our prayers and praises would continue in spite of disruptions.

Soon afterwards Tony was with us in a small prayer meeting and for about an hour we courageously ignored his bellowing and thrashing about. Suddenly, in the midst of a gentle song of love and praise, the noises ceased. The poor man was exhausted but he was in possession of himself again. We continued our prayers and in fervent thanksgiving gave praise for his deliverance. Grinning sheepishly, he joined us.

In later conversation the root of Tony's spiritual bondage was exposed. The truth was that until then he had no testimony of Christ. Tony had not been able to talk with me about his personal experiences of Christ because of the inevitable intrusion of convulsions. Now he could. He had been repelled by the idea of a God who could suffer and give so

34

much importance to death. It had not occurred to him that Jesus' death had been for his sin. In fact, sin was an insignificant concept in his beliefs; it meant no more than breaking fasts, missing prayers and failures in ascetical perfection. He had been chasing spiritualist philosophies all his adult life and his god was a vague and impersonal embodiment of the mental peace he himself lacked.

In the hope of being released from torment Tony sought to be baptized with the Spirit at an independent full gospel meeting held by a visiting Episcopal priest. He was filled with a spirit, a religious spirit, I suspect—one that spoke in unknown tongues—but it was unclean.

After our conversation about the blood of Jesus, Tony's strange behavior stopped. Once in a while his stomach muscles quivered during the singing of praises but his shaky voice was the only evidence of it. He was free from strange spiritual manifestations and from mental illness, free and fluent in a beautiful gift of tongues.

He was free.

In September 1965 Tony moved into a core household of the community and became fully a part of us. In time he was a humble, gentle servant of Christ among His brethren, a gifted teacher of children.

A Needy Family

Myra was the first of the Smathers family to come for help.

Then the others, Chester and the four living children, loomed into sight and we had a problem family on our hands.

After eight years and five children she was threatening to leave him—or was it that she planned to find a lover? I had difficulty taking the threat seriously because in the depth of her depression she was such an unattractive woman.

My contact with Myra came through Doctor Bob Eckert. When Bob sold his medical practice in Galveston County and

35

moved to the Eastwood section of Houston, he found an opening on the staff of a small independent health clinic in a nearby Mexican district. Parkview clinic was Anglo-owned and operated and served many non-Latin patients, but besides its industrial insurance practice (employment physicals and employee health checks) it was supported chiefly by surrounding neighbors. Most of these were neither the indigent poor who were given government-supported free care nor more affluent Americans able to bear the full cost of private medical care. They were the struggling poor and the near-poor. To cater to these lower-income patients the clinic managed to stay alive by operating in an economic no man's land on the verge of bankruptcy. When the welfare plans of Medicare and Medicaid became established health programs, clinics such as Parkview lost many of their clients. Now that they had adequate insurance coverage many poor looked to the clinics of those who could afford the best, leaving Parkview to the top half of the near-poor who by themselves were unable to support them. Bob's salary was miserly in comparison with his income in private practice, but Parkview was a rich mine of evangelism and he was busy working it at peak load. Recently the Smathers had been brought to the surface.

Myra's chief physical difficulty was her weight. She was more than just fat; she was obese. From her waist down she was enormous—about ninety inches girth at the thighs. There was a glandular problem of course, possibly diabetes, but medication was purposeless without proper food intake. And Myra was incapable of controlling her diet because most of the time she was too depressed to remember, or so she claimed. Her hair was greasy blonde and hung in stringy ringlets about her ears, making a round face rounder; her skin was blue-veined and delicate, blending unnoticed into a smudge about the neck of her faded dress. Like the children's, her knuckles and elbows were grimy. And like the children, she had dozens of scarlet-rimmed, blue black sores on her legs caused by flea bites that were infected from scratching.

36

Chester was pitiful: bewildered-looking and helpless in her control. He loved her and she knew it. He first met me in my office along with the rest of his family, but I can recall the direct sound of his soft-spoken voice no more often than a half dozen times during the first year. When he and Myra addressed each other directly, things progressed peaceably until Chester's blank stare warned Myra that he disagreed with her. She would suddenly fuss with the children—their clothes, their hair, their toys, anything. Within moments they were unnerved and screaming. Then Myra used one of two tactics. Either she assumed a look of extreme depression and became silent so Chester was compelled to pacify the frenzied children, or she herself became overly solicitous of their needs and played on the floor like one of them. In either event, Chester's opposition was averted and the controversial subject avoided. Chester was unlikely to raise the issue again soon.

One might wonder about Myra's motives for such behavior. What was to be gained? Nothing really. She had been married as a sixteen-year-old immature girl, and now she was a twenty-four-year-old immature woman. Unfortunately her ineffectual husband doted on her and the children.

The Smathers were poor. Chester was doing his best as a mechanic's apprentice, receiving lower wages than the minimum standard. Neither he nor Myra could manage their children, their income or themselves. And Myra had given up trying after the death of their third child.

It happened in a bath tub a few years earlier. Myra, not yet twenty, was giving two of her three children an afternoon bath. She had drawn water to a depth of only an inch or two, then after testing it for comfort she sat her one-year-old baby in the tub, stood a two-year-old sister beside her and gave stern but idle instruction about caring for the baby. Then Myra went outside to chat over the fence with a neighbor. In a few minutes the older child came screaming to her mother; inside was a mind-shattering scene. Unsatisfied with the depth of her bath water, the older child had innocently turned on a spigot. The water was scalding and came out full force. Vainly she attempted to turn it off, but her feet were burning so she crawled from the tub and ran naked to her mother. By the time Myra got to the bathroom her baby, helpless in the slippery tub, was beet-red—scalded and drowned.

The sight of her dead infant had not been eradicated from Myra's emotions. She blamed herself for being a poor mother, which by most standards she had become; and in self-condemnation she accused Chester of blaming her, though in his simple love he had not. She had grown to hate the life Chester offered her; but even worse, it felt like she hated him: too many bills, too little money, a child a year, and an unreasonable fear of leaving her growing pack unattended. She was trapped at twenty-four and wanted out.

But somewhere in the back of her mind, she knew Jesus. So did Chester. So we prayed and asked Jesus to straighten out their lives. In the presence of both of them, Bob and I told the Lord that the community was available for that purpose. After the prayer Bob asked the amount of their indebtedness. I assume he helped them take care of it, because it was not mentioned again.

Myra and the children continued to be a problem, sometimes well, sometimes not. Chester was a problem because his family was.

Then during the winter of 1966 the Smathers moved into Eastwood and became full community members. I suppose it was literally we who moved them, carload after carload, into a house our wives had made ready. After they moved, Myra and her children could be seen daily at the Eckert's—sewing, cooking and sharing. Nancy Eckert, a professional home economist, taught Myra about nutrition and child care, about shopping and homemaking, and about managing the house so they could live within Chester's income.

Myra lost weight and blossomed into a homespun beauty. The children grew healthy and clear-skinned.

Over the course of several years, through prayer and counsel in the midst of our love, Myra's memory of her baby's death was healed; and something happened in Chester. He set up a "shade tree" mechanic's shop beside their small frame house across from the church; in his spare time he made friends with every Volkswagon in the neighborhood.

By loving the Smathers and several other families like them, the community learned lessons about serving the underprivileged by being with them in their own homes. They were useful lessons later incorporated into community programs, when the parish addressed the needs of the neighborhood at large.

A Student's Wife

During my youth I was always conscious of the demands of a religious life and, not without a sense of pride, I attempted to live virtuously. My family was firmly entrenched in a popular denominational church, and though I see now that our own life together didn't attest to the love and peace of Christ, we supposed at that time that we lived more or less as Christians should. But the lack of belief, or rather the unbelief, gradually chipped away at my faith until in my late teens I decided that it was all an illusion.

Rebellion, quiet yet intense rebellion, came to be the essence of my life. I married at nineteen, while a sophomore in college, and moved to Houston where my husband attended medical school. Soon I realized how undisciplined I was in attempting to help support us, so I backed down on my premarital promise and insisted on returning to school. My disappointment in my marriage, in having quit school, in being pregnant, in my life in general was the impetus for a wholehearted escape into intellectualism. I literally poured myself out in the effort to learn all I could about all I could, neglecting my husband and baby daughter. Scholastic involvement preempted everything, and I gradually evolved

39

into a prideful, demanding woman, torn with insecurity and doubts, blinded by intellectualism. In swift succession I was divorced, entered graduate school, and remarried.

Gradually, the optimism of youth left me and was replaced with a growing concern about the reason for living. I saw the years ahead as no longer of any consequence. The sense of achievement appeared now as a vain and empty striving toward self-glorification. In a word, my days were just useless attempts to stave off fate or to forget it.

Out of a need to find something in which to believe, I began to search the writings of C. S. Lewis. I knew instantly that there was a sense of security engulfing me when I read his books. Simply because he was a member of the Anglican Church, I decided to attend the Episcopal Church nearest me in hopes of finding that same security. And, praise God! It was there in the Church of the Redeemer. I don't believe I heard much of the pastor's words for nearly a year, but I just sat, soaked up and clung to an indescribable feeling of safety. And, gradually, the Lord began to show me Himself and His reality in the lives of the people there.

Life is good now, because it isn't mine any longer. I feel safe because 1 am His, and His Spirit strengthens my faith in Him every day. This is my real calling. And I'm free! Free of pride, free of the falseness of my former desires; I'm free to love my family and to be no one. Thank you, Lord.

A Magdalen

Author's note:

Once at a Lenten covered-dish supper where I was guest preacher in a church near Redeemer parish, my eye was caught by a woman whose face looked tormented and snarled. I saw her briefly at a distance of about thirty yards. Actually she was not grotesque at all. I had seen something of her spiritual state, something under the surface of her skin.

After supper the rector of the parish took me to his home for coffee. We talked about the ministry of satanic forces at work in the church, and about the need for pastors to perfect the charisma for spiritual discernment. I told him of the woman I had glimpsed, but he seemed unimpressed by my suspicions because she was a recent convert being nurtured in one of his most successful witnessing groups. During our conversation a telephone rang and he left the room to answer it. In his absence I was strongly impressed to read what seemed in that setting a meaningless verse from scripture:

For as the crackling of thorns under a pot,
so is the laughter of the fools;
this also is vanity.

Ecclesiastes 7:6

The whole situation seemed odd. I had been strongly impressed by an aura of evil torment on the poor woman's face; now there was this rather laughable bit of scripture. Then I learned that the telephone call was from the very woman I had seen and described to my host. She was in distress and had called asking for prayer. Her startled pastor said we would be at her home as quickly as possible.

The distraught woman was alone and wringing her hands with anxiety when we arrived. She babbled about trying to sleep and about having vague fears, but I insisted on details. With difficulty she told me of a few nocturnal visits from some sort of ephemeral "presence" that to her was so real she had once run screaming with fright from her bed. On some occasions after this presence had left her she was overwhelmed by a horrible disgust. Once her vagina burned unbearably for an hour as a result of "its" visitation. There had been such a visitation that night and she was almost inconsolable.

I was not satisfied about her spiritual condition. She was evasive about my question concerning salvation. So finally I said simply, "——, what do you think of the cross, and the blood Jesus shed for our sins?"

She giggled—a brittle, crisp noise. I was amazed at how like the burning of dry twigs it sounded.

Again I inquired, "Do you believe all your sins are under the blood of Jesus,——?" Again the dry laughter.

She could converse about anything but the blood of Jesus!

Recalling the verse from Ecclesiastes, I concluded that, even though she claimed membership in a witnessing group, she was probably not yet free from what her life had been filled with in the past. I gave her some chapters from scripture to read, claimed her for the kingdom of Christ and prayed she would catch a vision of the cross of Jesus, finding release, safety and comfort there.

This is her story.

We were small-town farm folk, but when I was seven my parents, for some reason, moved to the city. Dad went wild—drinking and women—and when I was nine they were divorced. Various aunts and uncles came and kept us (one brother, one sister and myself) while my mother worked, but I always seemed to myself to have been a loose object not really connected to anything.

At age twelve I was full-grown of body and discovered boys.

I had a friend named Bell who had a boyfriend who had a friend. I sneaked out the window to see the friend and ended up married to him (he thought I was eighteen). Mother put a quick end to that, and since he was duped he was set free, but I was sent to the Convent of the Good Shepherd for eleven months. The convent is where I met my friend Evelyn.

In my relationships with boys, the lead-up was always a beautiful thing to me; for the first time in my life I felt loved. Then when the boy started to demand what he had been leading up to, I would be brokenhearted. I would hate to have to count all the times and places I had to walk home, protecting my "honor."

Then there was that boy who was old enough to talk marriage and "taking me out of all that" and "Of course we'll wait if you insist, but a man has certain needs and if you don't I'll have to go somewhere else." Well, that did it. There was no longer any "honor" left—only shame and feeling dirty all the time. He was eighteen and his parents found out what he was up to. His father threatened him with a baseball bat if he so much as spoke to me again. I was fourteen and my friend Evelyn said I was better off. Anyway she had a boyfriend who had a friend.

Her friend's friend was Earl and he turned out to be not so bad.

Earl was taking goofballs (a narcotic sometimes called yellow jackets) and offered me one. I was horrified but Evelyn knew what to say: "Leave her alone, she's just a baby." So I took the pill and woke up sometime the next morning with Evelyn knocking on the door. I married Earl. He was twenty-seven years old and had just been released from prison for manslaughter.

Earl and his friend made a living by stealing. We never bought groceries; everything was "boosted." I never will forget the first time I went to the store with them. I bought what was needed, went home, and this fellow opened his coat and took about twenty dollars worth of groceries out of his clothes—I'd never seen him take a thing. At night they would go out and rob places. All the time I was getting more and more involved with narcotics, pills and marijuana.

At first it was pleasing for Earl to have a fourteen-year-old "pig" to show off, but then the city got tight and more and more of their friends were getting caught. They got afraid to go out on "jobs" so they started looking around for a safe way to get money without working. Evelyn and I were it. At first it was just going in places drinking with men and conning them out of money. We tried street walking, but that was too dangerous. Earl called a porter friend of his in one of the downtown hotels and we were in business—except the first man they sent me to was a reprobate. I ran, shoes in hand—no more prostituting for me. I guess by now Earl had in his own way become attached to me because he said, "OK." We moved in with mother and he got a job as a longshoreman; but I had no feeling for him except fear and when he gave me money to find us an apartment I took it and went to my dad's. In the three months I was there, I saw him sober three times. He was already an alcoholic.

I don't even remember how exactly I got back in the middle of the character world, but soon I found myself back in a pill habit. I went for weeks not knowing what was going on, waking up in strange places with strange faces.

Then there was the one who tried to straighten me up so I would be of dollar value. I sort of came to for this one and immediately had to be in love. I thought I was pregnant. He was out of town with a friend. I called the friend to find out where he was, and told the friend to tell him he was going to be a papa. I never heard from him again. But the friend said he would help me. He paid for a hotel room and introduced me to a porter so I could make enough money to get started somewhere else. I took an overdose of pills and he came and got me and took me to my mama. After I got my strength back he said, "I work at this cab stand, see. I'm a night dispatcher and I bootleg whiskey and make good money on my own. We can get you an apartment with a phone and— well, you know the rest." I was a call girl for some time.

During this time I tried to kill myself twice. I wouldn't be making enough money to suit him, or I would stay gone longer than he thought I should and he'd beat me. I wasn't pregnant before, but now I was and I had to have an abortion. I left town because the character world was much more organized then and I couldn't have gone anywhere without being found out. At that time I was a valuable piece of property—as much as one hundred dollars a night. I went to Dallas and don't know how I found the character center but I did. The same routine—back hard on pills—new man—"Let me take you out of all this"—same old line—back to prostitution. I couldn't take anyone back home to mama because I didn't fit in there any more. I left and got hooked up with safecrackers. I married one of them so I wouldn't have to testify against him. He went to prison anyway and his aunt sent me through business college.

Then I met the strong silent type—"a square." He promised the good life, a home and all that jazz, so I divorced the one in prison. I told "all" to this one, who married me anyway. But he always had contempt. There were so many, many reasons it just couldn't work. I needed his constant reassurance that he loved me, and any show of affection was to him a show of weakness. I tried to get pregnant but couldn't. We separated and I found I *was* pregnant. I had the child, then we went back together for the child's sake, but things were worse, not better. We divorced and I went home to mother. I got married again, but it was a war of the sexes right from the beginning and two more children came along right away. We hated each other, but were held together by the children and the knowledge that neither one of us could live alone; it was unbearable. In those days I walked always on the edge of a dark, deep pit, and just one little push—or too much relaxing—and I would fall into an eternity of darkness . . . screaming, screaming, screaming.

We began separately to find a way to live together. He turned to drinking and staying with the boys. I don't much blame him; I wasn't very good company in those days. We agreed that we should find a church to rear the kids in, so I looked for one. He said I could go the first Sunday and if it didn't hurt me he would go too. So I went and felt right at home the minute I walked in the door.

My husband went the next Sunday and liked it, so we started in confirmation classes. He didn't find many men in

45

the church but I had better luck; we had several prayer groups for women. As I began to see the Lord in these people I only knew they had something I wanted. Suddenly I had a sampling of the Lord's peace and began attending the witness meetings regularly. Life was beautiful. Then some strange things began to happen. I began to lose my peace and would go for nights without sleeping. I would go to witness meetings, get my peace back, then lose it again. Sometimes a terrible fear would come. Once I felt someone in the car with me so strongly that I turned to see who was there, and there wasn't anybody.

During Lent, Graham Pulkingham spoke at our church and afterwards went home with our rector. He told our rector that there was a woman in our parish who was demon possessed and described her to him. Our rector said it sounded like me but that it couldn't be me because I was a witnessing Christian. Just then his phone rang and it was me begging him to come out. I needed help badly. This thing had manifested itself to me and in fear I was shaking as though in a seizure. He and Graham came. Graham saw I wasn't born again, bound the thing and gave me scriptures to read to put me under conviction. Oh my, was I! I cried for days—couldn't face anyone. Just when I thought surely I was going to die, the Lord came in. It was misting rain, but to me it was the most beautiful day in my whole life. I ran outside, chased the dog, he chased me, my heart just full of sheer joy and love.

My whole outlook on life changed. Before, church was a place to drop the kids and be with the adults for a while; now it was where my Lord was. But sometime later I had to face the fact that I was far from being a real disciple. While my outlook had changed, my self had not. I found that I had the same weaknesses as before, except that now they were unbearable in the face of the beauty of the Lord. I fell into a pit of self-condemnation that I was only rarely able to crawl out of. I called Graham finally and he said that I needed the

46

Lord's fullness. Tuesday night at the prayer meeting I found myself asking for "the fullness of the Lord," having no earthly idea what that meant, and I was somewhat shocked to discover that this involved the gift of speaking in tongues. I didn't know whether anything had happened or not. When I got home there came a sentence in my head that sounded an awful lot like Latin to me. I went on as before, afraid to go back to the Redeemer.

The Lord allowed me to go into the pit. While I was there He was able to show me what was in the place and also what a hold these things had on me. Soon I ran, not walked, to the Redeemer. I had to be there. Now I sought to accept baptism with the Holy Spirit. While they were praying for me, Graham commanded the fear and the lust and the lies to leave me. Jealousy left too. Then I found myself crying out to the Lord to sent the Comforter. All of a sudden I was—what can I say?—"in the Spirit" at the cross, no longer crying for me but for the broken figure there; not that I saw Him with my eyes, but I saw Him and I beseeched Him to call my name so that I could come to Him, to help Him. Then He gave me a sentence in a heavenly language.

The Lord began to show me that the natural love I had for my family was at best "sick." It started with my husband—resentment, anger, at times pure hatred would come to the surface. The Lord showed me that I was now a servant in my own house for Him. Not only was my position that of a servant, but I could expect nothing in return from my family; the Lord was my employer. Oh my, how bitter this was to me—especially regarding my husband. I spent days on my face crying out to the Lord to deliver me from these feelings, because I didn't want Him to turn me away.

Bless Him, He delivered me. As I truly tried to love my husband for the Lord's sake, He blessed it and gave me a love in my heart, a pure joy in doing the thing that pleased my husband.

The Lord is doing wonders in my family since we moved

closer to the church. He's arranging this household in His own way and is establishing it in His peace and giving us such a deep trust in Him. Praise His holy Name!

My ugliness is so much more than I've been able to express here, and the Lord's love to me is so much more wonderful, but perhaps this outline's enough to give a small picture of how merciful our God has been to me.

Newlyweds

Although one of us had been born again for a decade and baptized in the Spirit about a year before we met, the other was unaware of his need for a vital relationship with the living God. Be that as it may, the Lord had work to do to prepare us both for this walk of faith to which we had been called.

Before our marriage we attended Redeemer regularly during the months of getting acquainted. In addition to the Word being preached on Sundays, the Friday night Bible study indeed fed us; the scriptures had never before been so revealed, spreading out before us the mysteries of God—His love, His power, and sweetest of all His very presence among us. No wonder there was that deep hunger within us to abide here!

So we were married and I became Mrs. Abbott in this place among these people we had come to love so well. We were then only vaguely aware of an uncertain demand upon us, one we were eager to fulfill once it was recognized. For the next ten months we went about the task of learning to live together, still on the fringes of what was obviously an encampment of the Lord. During those days the insurance industry and teaching profession commanded our attention and occupied almost every evening. But there were still Friday nights and Sundays, and that vague demand persisted until it began to take form. We lived seventeen miles from the neighborhood where Redeemer is located. Our apartment just happened to be in the growing section of Houston, the one reputed to have the best schools, the best opportunities for families, homes; in short, the best the world had to offer two people getting started. We entertained thoughts of a home in this area and went so far as to take care of preliminaries toward the purchase of one. It was then that we realized the Lord was confronting us with a choice.

Our hearts really longed for the life we witnessed on Fridays and Sundays. Now, were we willing to pay the price? Were we willing to forego the new side of town for the old, two salaries for one, the reasonable assurance of a predetermined pattern of living for one that in no way could be planned even for the moment at hand? In other words would we trust the Lord to show us a new way to walk, one without plans for tomorrow. Praise the Lord for the living testimonies of all the saints who had already made their decisions to move into the church neighborhood! There really was no decision to make, for the Lord had by now worked in both of us the desire to follow Him. With hopeful hearts we sought wisdom from our elders in the community concerning our place in this body, praying fervently that He wanted us here where we so wanted to be. In the quiet, dim coolness of the chapel what had once been vague became clear. He had called us to be here in this place at this time. Our hearts said, "Amen." And there was a vision, too, something about spring onions that were being divided and whose outer layers were being stripped away.

All this took place in 1966, when our clear calling together as a community began to be reality in terms of a day-to-day walk. There was the summer youth program with its various work projects involving many families of the fellowship; those who had worked in it together all day joined with those who hadn't been able to be with us, and we shared the evening meal—one hundred fifty of us. Afterwards there were songs of praise and thanksgivings and sharing in the Word. Imagine, learning to live and work with the entire fellowship and walking together in love—learning to give place to one another. There was the necessity of learning to share with whomever the Lord sent, and even give away what the world calls yours—your home, your possessions, your time, your self—and to do so in love.

There was a lot of learning how to submit to the Lord's guidance into places of ministry where we had little or no talent and sometimes less taste. We saw His power perform miracles both in situations and in us, so that there was no doubt whose work it really was, or who was really doing it. Distaste and doubt became replaced with a joy and an eagerness to do whatever pleased Him; there was love for the work, a love that we knew was not our own.

Then came the call to put aside the security of a job that was known and understood—but for what? For ministry? Yes. But which one—a pastor? That seemed far outside the realm of known capabilities. What does "ministry" mean? Then the Lord began to teach and train us in a service that is in keeping with a scripture that one day He had given Gordon: "Lay not up for yourselves treasures upon earth . . . seek ye first the kingdom of God, and His righteousness . . . Sufficient unto the day is the evil thereof" (Matt. 6:19,33, 34, KJV). In less than a year and a half the insurance industry became a thing of the past. Parish Administrator. That was the ministry in which those exhortations in Matthew could be put to the test in us.

Spring onions! Looking back, those onions have a significance that they never had before! Praise the Lord! He's doing what He said He would do, and how many layers have already been stripped away. How much separation from unnecessary infatuation with the world has already taken place. And yet how many divisions remain to be made? No matter, because, "We know whom we have believed, and are persuaded that He is able. . . ."

When I was seventeen years old I was living in California and I got arrested for needle marks and drug addiction and was placed with the California Youth Authority. While they had me I started going to church and was trying to rehabilitate myself so that when I came home I'd just be a good guy. I never really thought much about becoming a Christian; that was something for old people or squares. So I came home and did real good for about two or three days. I guess being locked up a little over a year didn't seem to bother me all that much because I got in trouble right away.

Soon I got married, thinking that would solve my problems—I'd at least get away from home that way. We stayed married a couple of months and then I woke up one morning in jail again—two counts of mischievous felony. The minister that married us (my wife had called him) was more or less using my theory: he just wanted me to be a good guy, stay out of trouble and everything. He never told me, "What you need to do is fall on your knees and ask God to come into your life."

When I was released, I was placed on parole in California. Things hadn't changed. It seemed every other weekend I'd wind up in jail. I just kept falling right back down, but I'd come out with more determination to do good this time. I couldn't keep a job. Finally I realized that I was married, had two kids, used narcotics, couldn't work, and needed money for my habit. I broke into a place, got caught, and was sentenced to four years in the Texas Department of Correction.

While I was there I was a big blank, just taking up the space, but my mother died and I came home on reprieve for the funeral. I couldn't understand how a loving God could take my mother whom I loved so much. Just before that I came up for parole but only got a year cut off my sentence. I asked myself, "What would you have done if you had made parole?" I said, "Well, I know I'd go back to Houston and I would smoke a little weed and shoot a little heroin and drink all the beer. . ." And I said, "This is what got me into this place; I don't want this the rest of my life." So I started going to group therapy, and I went to school trying to get a GED [General Education Diploma], and Wednesday nights I went to a Bible class in the chapel. You got points if you went to this—you had to have points to make parole—I knew this looked *real* good, so I started going. All the time I was trying to rehabilitate myself I wasn't looking for Christ, wanting to become a Christian, wanting to be saved.

Finally I made parole and came home. Before I got to the bus station that day I had four different chances to buy women or alcohol. I wanted to. I was real tempted and I wanted to, but I didn't, because I never could drink a half pint of whiskey or a couple of beers and go on about my business; I'd wind up getting drunk.

I hadn't been home very long before things started going wrong and got worse than they ever were before. I wound up in jail again, and the chances of going back to the penitentiary were great. They let me out on parole. Even though the parole officer was coming around, I still did all those things. But I knew I wasn't supposed to do them so I went to California for three months and stayed drunk all the time. I thought I had to. I thought I had to have something to drink before I could go to sleep at night because I hated myself. I hated looking in the mirror in the morning.

I came back to Houston and my wife, who had accepted Jesus, was living at the Ringos'. She told me if I'd live with one of the families in the fellowship of the Church of the Redeemer and show how I could straighten up, she and the kids would come back to me. She wanted me to go to Dr. Eckert's house. I said, "I don't want to live with those people! I don't have anything in common with them. I'd be bored the whole time I was there." She asked me just to try

52

it. That was on a Tuesday and I'd just found a job that day, so I said, "I'll go over there and make a payday and then if I don't like it, I'll move out."

In California I had been staying with my cousin and his wife. They have four kids and he drank a lot, too. While I was at the Eckerts' I wasn't drinking anything, so I had a lot of time to think with a clear mind. I could remember what my cousin's family was like, because of the drinking and what-have-you, and mine wasn't any different. Then I could look around and see the Eckerts' and I thought, "This is the way I want my family to be." I thought that if I could just be "good" I would make it. But I know now there wasn't any chance of that.

I was in the service one Friday night. After the service was over and they had an altar call I said, "I think I'll go outside and smoke a cigarette." So I went outside and lit the cigarette. The Lord was dealing with me, but I still wanted to shut him off. Well, I couldn't even smoke the cigarette it tasted so bad, so I came back in the church and asked my wife, "What do they do when you go to the altar? Do they just pray for you?" She said, "Yes." And I said, "Well let's go down there and let them pray for us." So I went down and knelt at the altar. It was real easy. I thought it would be hard—especially for me as much as I'd done. I didn't think that God really loved me. But all I had to say was, "Here I am, I know I'm a sinner, but I want to be saved." Some of the elders started praying and I don't think my feet touched the floor 'til the time I got back to my seat.

There's been a complete change in Betty's and my life; the kids are different and even my job's been affected. I have a love for people now that I didn't have before—a concern for them. I'm real happy. I don't have any trouble sleeping at night. And I don't have to worry about trying to be good because now I am good—well, to me it's so easy and every-thing. I wish everybody could be this happy.

53

I have always loved the church. My doll and I were regular attenders before I could talk, and the *Book of Common Prayer* was my first reader. In our small West Texas mission church there was a gentle British nurse who patiently used to point out each word of the services, and words like "inestimable" felt more familiar to me than "Dick" and "Jane."

An understanding that life in the church was everybody's responsibility came easily then—we had no "professionals" to lean on. Every other Sunday my father read a published sermon, and on alternate Sundays he read the prayers. Baptisms and funerals were the bishop's business and we saw him often. The sense of responsibility for parish life engendered by this mission situation was probably not a common one: all of us shared the ministry. Even we children had a part. My sense of belonging in the life of the church began with the care exercised by those parishioners for each other. Not only were they parishioners; they were the people I felt at home with.

It seemed as though I never would turn twelve. That was the age for confirmation, but after my importunate pleading and my parents' assurance that I knew what I was doing the day of confirmation was allowed when I was only eleven. Since we had no vicar the organist, a woman of faith, prepared me for that event. Exactly what she taught escapes me, but Ena McQueen gave liberally of herself and reinforced in me a growing desire to offer myself to the Lord "whose service is perfect freedom"—whatever that meant. I wanted to be as much a part of the church as possible.

There were several questions that popped in and out of my mind during the years that followed; questions about our sins and the general confession saying that "the burden of them is intolerable." I thought I should feel that way, but frankly I didn't. How could you love the Lord with "*all* thy heart, and *all* thy soul, and *all* thy strength"? I didn't even know where to begin, but something inside of me wanted to.

By the time I was in high school my family had moved to Texas' Gulf coast and to a large parish. The closeness between our family and the parish church continued—we changed our dinner time during Lent to attend daily evening services—and when time came to think about a career, full time work in the church was a natural consideration for me. As a little girl I had wanted to be a priest until it struck me that they were all men. Marrying a priest would have done nicely, but that opportunity never presented itself, so with the help of our rector I made long-range plans to enter the field of Religious Education.

One day in the last term of high school an acquaintance asked if I were interested in joining an ecumenical study group. There was an odd assortment of seven of us who joined and found an openness in sharing that I had never known I longed for until then. For the first meeting we discussed our feelings about the Lord's Supper. Things got off to a serious start when one boy opened himself to describe an experience during communion some weeks earlier which had changed his life. We had all known him to be a hoodlum and the depth of his experience with the Lord served to melt away some of our inhibitions and defenses. A small community was born. From that first meeting we were honest and forthright in ways none of us had ever known and that was an experience of the church I wanted to keep.

We grew together until fall, when we separated to enter different colleges. The fervency we knew faded, and new grown-up experiences had a better definition, but I ached to be part of a community of openness and mutual concern. Having a ready shoulder and a willing ear, I was one of those people others seemed to come to with their problems. The answers they sought were to be found in the context of the church, I believed, but I had no idea how to help find them.

55

In fact I needed them then for myself. How could I seriously consider a career in Religious Education unless I found some better thing to offer than what I had? I set out in search of a church where something real was happening so my conscience could be at peace.

I was neither frantic nor unreasonable. I went searching like a sensible Episcopalian. There were study groups and Bible courses, and there was Bill Clebsch's course in "The Mission of the Church" at Austin's Episcopal seminary. Mostly, however, I went from church to church looking for someone whose gospel could make the difference in the lives of those who needed it. I never found that church in Austin.

My first job was in Houston editing medical manuscripts at M. D. Anderson cancer hospital. The work was fascinating, and my apartment was shared with three good friends from college. We settled in to explore life outside the academic community. It was great. But I was still unsettled about the church because Houston churches seemed no different from the ones in Austin. Each Sunday I visited a different parish, still looking for a community of people who felt at home with each other and whose life and message was meaningful in the face of need.

One day I had occasion to telephone a friend. I was considering buying season tickets to the Houston Symphony and thought of her because she was a musician; Nancy had just been hired to develop a string program in one of Houston's suburban school systems. She was looking for an apartment of her own but in the meantime was staying with her sister and brother-in-law, Betty Jane and Graham Pulkingham.

Our conversation was brief because she had already purchased her tickets, but after suggesting that I phone to see if the seats next to hers were taken, she asked pointedly, "Where are you going to church, Arabella?"

"Oh, I've been trying one place and then another looking for somebody who's preaching something real."

"You ought to come over here to Graham's church. The

Holy Spirit's moving in a wonderful way," she suggested guardedly.

I had no idea what she meant by "moving in a wonderful way," but I decided to find out. Besides, I remembered a friend of mine suggesting once that if I ever wanted to talk to a priest I should call Graham Pulkingham. That was when he was at St. David's in Austin. I could never corral my thoughts into sensible enough questions to ask a stranger, so Graham Pulkingham had remained only a name to me.

The following Sunday after a half-hour trip on the freeway I arrived at Church of the Redeemer. The service was the only thing that felt familiar. There were no windows and my attention was coerced into contemplating a mural dominated by a figure of Jesus brilliantly spotlighted behind the altar. The nave was four-fifths empty and hardly anyone but myself sang or said a word.

The liturgy progressed like any other Service of Holy Communion until time for the sermon. One thought from it remains locked in my memory. "You go to movies and cry your eyes out over the difficulties in other people's lives; but have you ever wept because the sin in your own life offends the heart of God's love? You go to football games and shout your head off—cheering until you're hoarse; but have you ever shouted for joy because you know God's forgiveness?—and because you are *sure* of your relationship to Him as His son?"

The answer on both counts had to be No. But I knew I had heard *something* that could make a difference. I knew that, in spite of the mural, Redeemer was going to be my new church home.

After the service Nancy, who was a member of the choir, introduced me to Graham and Betty Jane and showed me around the dingy and ill-kept property. Since the choir could obviously use more voices I promised Nancy I would attend a rehearsal on the following Wednesday night.

We had tea at the rectory after rehearsal so it was quite late by the time I returned home to find a long-distance phone message to call my parents. My brother John had been in an automobile accident the night before. Our birthdays are eighteen months apart, but we had grown up like twins. The news of his accident was shattering to me, not because of fear of physical injury but because this seemed like another in a seemingly endless succession of bad breaks for him. He had been subjected to being "Arabella's brother" in school, a boy mostly interested in sports following one year behind a sister who was an honor student, and it seemed as though every time he started in a new direction something backfired. Now he would lose his new job, after quitting college and starting work in order to pay debts incurred during a marriage that had ended in divorce a few weeks before. In some perverted way, I guess I thought my happiness was stealing John's from him because I felt guilty that he was in trouble again and life was so easy for me.

At the time I was not certain what John's injuries amounted to, but I made plans to go to his hospital room in Louisiana after work on Friday. The next morning, Thursday, I became hopelessly distracted thinking about John and by noon decided to spend the lunch hour alone just driving around in my car. The car almost drove itself to Redeemer Church, and in the basement chapel I prayed seriously, "Lord, if you have to strike me dead do it, but please heal John."

The time had moved so swiftly that I would have to hurry in order to be back at work on time, so I rushed up the stairs from the chapel to the street. Either the car's starter was broken or the battery was dead, because when I turned the key in the ignition nothing happened—absolutely nothing. Frightened at the thought of being late returning to my new job and having no idea what to do for the car, I ran in search of help. At that very moment Nancy's brother-in-law was coming out of the church. Was he "Father," "Mister" or simply "Graham"?

"Oh, Graham Pulkingham," I called, flustered and foolish, "can you help me?"

When I told him my plight, he admitted to very limited knowledge about automobiles himself, but there was a friend at the rectory who might be able to help. The friend set out for my car with jumper cables, but before he had a chance to use them Graham and I walked up.

"Let me just see if it will start," Graham said.

It started instantly.

On our way to the car I had blurted out my concern for John, so when the car started at Graham's touch I thought, "*Now* he'll think I made up the whole car story just for a chance to tell him my troubles." Embarrassed, I apologized for the inconvenience and hurried into my car.

Graham leaned and gave me a fatherly kiss on the forehead saying, "Arabella, the Lord made your car stall so I'd know what to pray for."

This was one of the strangest men I had ever met.

"The Lord made your car stall. . . ." Indeed! That's absurd—or is it? All afternoon the thought plagued me. Does God really interfere with mundane affairs like that? He's supposed to be holy; what's He doing messing with my car? Over and over the phrase hounded my thoughts, "The Lord made . . ."

At suppertime I stayed away from my apartment, giving a shopping trip as the excuse, when in truth I wanted to be alone and think about the strange things that were going on. Once again the car drove itself to the church. There in the basement chapel, Graham and some others were celebrating an intimate service of Holy Communion so I slipped into the back pew. I felt welcomed and at home. For the first time in years tears were set free and something childlike was released in my pent-up spirit. They were not exactly tears about John; there was no single reason for the weeping but there it was—quiet, gentle—until the service ended and everyone left.

In an empty chapel my weeping continued unchecked for about an hour.

Faraway, muffled voices were sounding in a room down the hallway. Then a clatter of footsteps approached and the chapel door opened. Nancy entered and dropped to her knees beside me. In a few moments she asked, "How's your brother?" and I replied, "There's no further news."

We talked about John and my concern for him; we talked about Nancy and the things that were happening in her. Nancy talked about the Lord and at one point she said, "Arabella, the Lord will speak to you if you'll just ask Him."

It had never occurred to me that just anyone could hear the Lord. I thought you had to be someone special for that to happen; so I asked, "How?"

"Different ways," she replied confidently. "If you don't know any other way just open the Bible, believing, and He'll speak to you there."

Never before had I heard Nancy Carr talk like that. She just wasn't the sort to be looking for answers in scripture or initiating conversation about the Lord. Something had happened in the six months since we had left college, and I sensed it was real. I took a Bible from the seat and prayed after she left. "Lord, if you really are there, please, speak to me." Allowing the pages to fall open upside down at II Kings 20:5, I turned the book upright and read, ". . . Thus says the Lord, the God of David your father: I have heard your prayer, I have seen your tears; behold, I will heal you; on a third day you shall go up to the house of the Lord."

The next day after work I drove to my brother's sickbed in Louisiana and learned that some internal complications which the doctors had been unable to control had disappeared the night before. Hearing that news only put the exclamation point on the quiet knowledge that God had indeed spoken to me. I made no exuberant outbursts about the things that were happening; as a matter of fact I shared them with no one; but I was overwhelmed with silent wonder.

For the next several Sundays I drove home to Houston in the very early morning having visited John over the weekend, and it was for me a journey to "the house of the Lord,"

60

where I knew His presence among the people at Redeemer Church.

Soon I was on the phone asking Graham if he needed help with a scout troop or the Junior Altar Guild. I was looking for some way to get involved. He suggested I come the following Tuesday to a "little meeting" in the choir room, after which we could talk about it.

That "little meeting" turned out to be a room full of people singing almost every sentimental hymn in the 1940 Hymnal and we listened to a man they called "Brother" Frid teach from the Bible. His unsophisticated, black and white approach to the scriptures irritated my rational sensibilities to the point of anger, but I admired the confidence of his faith. There was something more than mere Bible worship in these people; they simply believed God.

At the close of the meeting we sang a hymn and went to the chapel for prayers. After the others had gone Graham and I talked—not about Girl Scouts and Junior Altar Guild, oddly enough. He told me of his trip to New York and his baptism with the Holy Spirit, things I had never heard of before but had no reason to doubt. Then he said, "When you ask the Lord to baptize you with His Spirit, Arabella, will you let Betty and Nancy and me pray with you?" Neither of us questioned I would eventually seek baptism with the Spirit; in fact I was ready to ask at that moment, but since Graham had said "when" it seemed not to be the time.

The time arrived the following week after the Tuesday night meeting. I had gone to the altar rail to offer a prayer of thanksgiving for my brother's rapid recovery. When that prayer was over a dozen people stood about me, and Brother Frid explained the matter of the gift of the Spirit. We prayed and although nothing obvious happened, when Graham asked, "Have you received, Arabella?" I nodded "Yes." I figured that since they had prayed for me, I must surely have received.

Then Brother Frid said, "Now when the Spirit comes,

61

Arabella, He comes bearing gifts. One of them is the gift of unknown tongues. Do you want to receive it?" I thought some years back to a time when my father had come home from a vestry meeting reporting that Episcopalians in California were doing something like that. My mother expressed her disapproval but my only thought was, "If the Bible talks about it, why not?" I had the same response to Brother Frid's question, "If the Bible talks about it, why not?" So we prayed that I would speak in tongues.

Once again I felt no different—my mouth remained shut, my tongue was still, my mind heard nothing strange. Everyone around me was praying in odd-sounding languages. It was beautiful. After a few minutes I was aware of being the center of interest, and I became fearful of keeping everyone late. "Apparently they intend to pray this way until I speak in tongues!" I thought, "the least I can do is oblige." It was then that I opened my mouth to make nonsense sounds which in a moment became spontaneous in the shape of a language. I was set free in praise, and something inside settled down.

There were no instant changes in my life, but a growing awareness of God's presence among us and continued evidences of His faithfulness caused a deepening of my devotion. I had found my self-offering in His "perfect service." I had found a "relevant" gospel—and a home.

That was autumn, 1964. In the spring of the next year we began gathering daily at 5:30 a.m. for prayer. One of the things our prayers produced was an idea for a summer program to help neighborhood children. Some came from Latin American families and there were serious language barriers to their learning. Others were from such a poor home environment that there was scant incentive to learn anything except what was necessary for survival.

One morning after the 5:30 gathering I stayed behind in the chapel to pray. It seemed unavoidable that the Lord was asking me to quit working for the summer and organize the children's program. That would mean resigning my job, there being no hope of a summer's leave, but surely such a thing would be crazy. While I was struggling, Graham came in and we talked. Seeing my confusion he said, "Arabella, let's pray and see if that doesn't help you understand things more clearly." We went to the altar rail where he laid his hand gently on my shoulder and began quietly praying in tongues. I joined him, and sometime during our prayer the confusion resolved itself into a clear vision of what the Lord wanted. That day I gave notice.

Life was a new adventure in many ways. I had been used to having money; now there was none. Suddenly I had become a full-time volunteer, living on my savings. That was eight years ago. Seven years and nine months after my savings ran out I am still a full time volunteer.

The Laborer

After twenty-five years a member of Redeemer Church I, John, finally gave myself to Him, the Redeemer, and He filled me to overflowing with His Spirit. Edith and I had been all stirred up about something, but we didn't understand it was the Lord wooing us until we talked to our pastor, Graham Pulkingham. He said we needed to be baptized with the Holy Spirit and something down inside of me said, "Amen," not even knowing what baptism with the Holy Spirit was all about. Then we were led to a Chinese-American Pentecostal church where we received the Spirit and all He brings. From then on He's truly been the Lord of my whole life. He's become my best companion and He's taught me to hear His voice.

For twenty-six years I was employed by the Houston Lighting and Power Company, and happily so. When I first started learning to walk with the Lord He said He wanted me to leave that job and serve Him at the church. I had everything a man could want—a dream house, three healthy kids, cars, money in the bank, a good job, and a wonderful wife.

Praise the Lord! When He spoke I had ears to hear and a heart to follow because by His grace I turned all my thoughts and everything else over to Him. In a few weeks I told my family and they were as happy as I was. But my fellow workers thought I was crazy; the boss had some reservations and asked me to stay on another month just to be sure. I tried to tell them I had nothing to do with the call or the answer. Like James and John when Jesus called them from fishing, I was drawn to Him.

All I want now is to be with Him every minute of every day. You know, to fellowship with Jesus; I just want to be the spitting image of Him. He has me doing lots of things with Him: teaching the Bible to the first-grade kids and new converts, counseling with folks about problems and needs, maintaining and keeping up the church property, repairs in the homes of all the saints around here—other things, too.

Every morning we have a time of Bible sharing at the church. Each one of us trusts the Lord to lead him to specific places in the scriptures and to show us something special He's saying for that day in those passages. Then we get together and as the Lord leads us, each one shares with everyone else what the Lord has shown him. Person after person shares fresh "light" from the Lord's Word. It's a miracle! These little bits and pieces of scripture fit together to make a beautiful lesson day after day. That's such a wonderful way to get new converts reading the Bible, too, and listening to the Lord. It's been my blessing to lead these sharing sessions since coming to the church to work.

And, oh yes, my work. He's a precious Lord to give me a job I like so much: cleaning up and fixing up everything that has got broken. And the wonderful men and boys I work with every day; they've been all messed up on dope or alcohol or something, and some of them hardly even know their own name any more. But working hard helps them along, and we pray with them and love on them when they get all out of sorts. The precious thing is the unity of mind and spirit that exists there. What a blessing it is to serve Jesus!

Author's note:
John's wife had been a member of Redeemer Church since she was a child. When the community began to form in 1964 her mother and father were among the "old-timers" still living in the parish neighborhood. Unable to understand why so radical a change must come about in their children's lives and why the familiar Episcopal religion was no longer good enough, these old-timers began complaining among themselves. Their dissatisfactions, though not mentioned to me, were aired before their children and their children's friends both in and out of the parish. John particularly was concerned that these oldsters spend their last years at peace with the Jesus whom he knew to be so precious. However, nothing appeased them; they magnified their hurt before anyone who would listen, and the situation was in danger of becoming a gossipy scandal.

One Sunday morning when the Eucharist was over and before anyone had left, I saw a commotion down front in the gospel side of the nave. Having followed the choir procession to the narthex I was a good distance from the disturbance, but it was clear that something of grave concern was going on. Instead of departing, the entire assemblage had moved without rubric or exhortation to its knees and was at prayer. The atmosphere sparkled with the sound of fervently lisping tongues as I hurried down a side aisle to where a small group was gathering.

As I approached I was suddenly struck by an immense force of supplication; I fell in a heap to my knees and wept. It was the sort of weeping that had happened to me only three or four times before and in each other instance a remarkable miracle or healing had ensued. I knelt on the floor for about ten minutes while the group before me leaned over a pew and ministered their concern to a situation that was still unidentified to me. Eventually an ambulance attendant arrived and carried John's mother-in-law out of the church.

Dr. Eckert was standing by me when the body was removed.

"You all right, Graham?" he asked.

"Yes," I replied, "what do you think about Mrs. Neville?"

"Heart attack, I guess. As far as I could tell she went out on the pew. No pulse, no heartbeat or evidence of breathing. Of course, I didn't have any instruments, but clinically she was dead."

That evening John told me what had happened in the ambulance. When they were a block or so from the hospital, the old woman sat bolt upright on the stretcher and demanded to know where she was. The attending physician at the emergency room when they got her there was irate. "What's this woman doing here; there's nothing wrong with her?" he demanded.

Old Mrs. Neville had been dead for about a half hour, but now she was alive!

A humorous after-effect of Mrs. Neville's resurrection was what happened to her neighbor and long-time friend, Mrs. Brown. Mrs. Brown left the church when she saw Mrs. Neville had passed away. She went home to her phone and spent several hours calling all over Houston spreading the unhappy news of Mrs. Neville's death.

By evening the Neville's phone was ringing off the wall with calls of sympathy for the bereaved old gentleman. Of course, Mrs. Neville answered the phone. Imagine the confusion!

After that time the Neville's complaining ceased, as did the grumbling of almost all the other oldsters. Somehow they were convinced that though unusual, something real was happening in the old Eastwood church.

My husband and I drank from the beginning of our marriage until he left me, pregnant with my youngest son, after a stormy twenty years.

We left the Lord out of our lives. There was one son we "dropped by" the church every Sunday because that seemed the right thing to do, but we never went with him. Much to our surprise, this son confessed Jesus Christ as his Savior when he was fourteen. My nephew was an assistant director in Youth for Christ and my husband and I were quite bitter toward him for "trying to make a preacher out of our boy."

During the next three years my drunken and adulterous life became so vile that I lost my home, my friends, my self-respect and my hope of ever living any other way. The only work I could find was in barrooms; my only concern was getting the next six-pack. Sometimes I wanted to get out from under all that filth and "be good." I thought that probably I ought to go to church, but never did it enter my mind that Jesus, not the church, would be my help. I was scared of dying and going to hell and sometimes my son and I talked about salvation, but I could never bring myself to accept Jesus as my personal Savior.

Some of the time I could manage to straighten up and live decently, but overall life was meaningless and empty for me. Although I was not divorced from my husband, I began to live with a man as his common-law wife. Ashamed of living in sin, I let my seven-year-old boy go to live with relatives who felt sorry for him. The son who knew Jesus was a freshman in college, and I had my three-year-old with me. The arrangement with this man was just like my marriage—hangovers, jealousies, quarreling, guilt feelings, nervousness, cigarette coughs—so one night during a party I tried to phone a sister who had helped me many times. Being unable to find her at home, I called her son, the Youth for Christ religious fanatic. All I could remember the next morning was that he had said he would come over and talk to me.

To my surprise, when he came he didn't "preach at" me or "pray over" me, but offered to take me to some people who could help. I was willing at the moment to do anything to change my ways, so we went to the Church of the Redeemer and talked with the pastor. He told me that if drinking was my problem, I should try Alcoholics Anonymous, but I had to admit that drinking was not really the problem. After explaining that the only way I could be helped was to forsake every vestige of this life and allow the Lord to make a new creature of me, he left for an appointment. At my request my nephew took me back to my apartment and as we drove he told me of person after person who had been set free by giving themselves to the Lord for His direction. When we got home I walked through the dreary apartment and looked at the refuse—all I had to show for twenty years of marriage— and realized that I could choose this or a Jesus who was not just a character in a book or a Savior who made my boy better, but a Jesus who was working miracles in people's lives *now*. I realized that I would never make it by myself and that Jesus wanted me. Suddenly I hated everything I saw of my life, and I walked out without even a change of clothes. Back at the church I knelt on the floor with several of the people there and asked Jesus to come into my life. When I got up there was no doubt that God had answered that prayer and I would never drink or smoke again. My entire body was cleansed from sin, and I was renewed by God's mercy and great love.

The Lord immediately began to set my life in order. Chiefly this consisted of medical care for my child, a place to live with a family whose lives were totally committed to the Lord, daily Bible studies and teachings, and constant fellowship with the saints.

A few weeks after my conversion my elderly mother became very ill and I visited her in the hospital. When I entered the room she gave no sign of recognizing me, but after I told her of the Lord's love recently shown in my life, and asked her to forgive me for the misery I had caused her, she rose up and shouted for joy. Two days later she was able to go home from the hospital—completely healed.

Soon after that my oldest son, home from college, went with me to the altar and we received the baptism with the Holy Spirit. When summer came my younger son returned home from my relatives, and I was reunited with my boys. We lived together in the home of a church family who were out of town for the summer. I had no job but we needed to be together, so the elders suggested I stay home with the boys for the summer and trust that the Lord would provide our groceries, clothing and other expenses; and the Lord provided in such abundance that soon we had two extra boys living with us. At the end of the summer we moved to a large house where young men of the church who are college students or who work on the church maintenance crew live upstairs. There was not a stick of furniture downstairs the morning we moved in, but before dark we each had a bed and before long it was beautifully furnished.

As the housemother and cook in a halfway house for men, I have seen many people come here seeking the Lord, or looking for release from some type of bondage such as dope addiction, alcoholism, mental illness or other afflictions. We have not always been victorious, but we have seen the Lord at work in every life that has come here. There is nothing else I want to do but serve and please Him.

An Organist

Most people came to the Church of the Redeemer seeking the Lord, but I came looking for a place to practice on a pipe organ. My husband had just received his Ph.D. in Zoology from Tulane University, and we, with our small son, had come to stay with my parents in Houston while he finished job interviews and settled on a position for the fall. When I heard that one of my music theory teachers, the wife of an

Episcopal rector, was now living in the city, I hoped I had found a place to practice. Since I am trained as an organist-director, the thought of having a whole summer with no place to play was not to my liking.

I heard before I came that this church was in some undefined way strange. They had just abolished all salaries for the music staff, and the rector believed the Holy Ghost talked to him. But I thought I could take care of myself, and after all, that had nothing to do with playing the organ there. I was wrong on both counts!

I went on Sunday, found my former teacher remembered me, and so I offered my services as summer substitute in return for practice privileges. Within two or three weeks I was playing on Sunday mornings for the main service. At this time my husband accepted a position which would move us to Illinois in September.

More and more I began to wonder just what was going on at that church. I really liked the people, even though they carried Bibles around most of the time and tried to sound like Psalm 150. One afternoon found me in the rector's office, telling him I wanted to talk to him about something, the exact nature of which I was unsure. I found out that what I wanted to hear was how the Holy Spirit can move into men's lives and cause Christianity and the church to come alive. There were certain parts of his testimony that I did not like at all (at my querying he admitted to speaking in tongues), but I clung to the thought that I was moving away in six weeks and so would be in no danger of really getting involved with these people.

After that conversation I knew without any doubt that the Lord wanted me to start going to the evening Bible study meetings twice a week. First I had a recital to play which took me out of town briefly, but then I started attending. I had a good idea of what the meetings were like before I came, but actually seeing and hearing it all was a shock. The singing was good; the testimonies were shattering; the Bible

70

study fascinating; and the prayer time in the chapel was absolutely frightening because I had no desire to hear people speaking in tongues.

The next days found me thinking of God constantly. In fact this was the only thing which kept me coming. My past life had been a struggle to know more of God, and in particular to be intimately aware of God; there were many days when He was far from my thoughts even though perhaps I might be playing pieces with religious titles, or practicing hymns and other service music. Now I seemed unable to concentrate on anything but God. I began to think that possibly these people were right in believing modern Christianity to be the same as early Christianity. After two weeks, I knew I needed to give in and ask for the baptism with the Holy Spirit. Stay or leave, I wanted to be turned into one of those funny people who love God more than the world and who talk about Jesus just as if He were beside them. One morning during my private prayers I asked to be baptized with the Holy Spirit and received immediately, very quietly.

From then on I felt that I was praying in tongues inside somewhere, but was unable to hear any actual words. A week or so of this convinced me there was no use in not wanting to do something outside that you kept on doing inside. It required the prayers of my brothers and sisters and the laying on of their hands before I could speak out, but the Lord was faithful. He gave me the gift of tongues and removed my fear of the prayer meetings.

However, there was another matter that needed to be dealt with before we moved to St. Louis. In one of Graham's sermons he said something about God not needing our talents; He needs only us. The thought seemed right, but I was offended. Several years out of my life and a great deal of hard work and money had gone into my training for church musicianship; I was proud of what I had to offer. Taking my offense to Graham I told him I could have little respect for a God who would be so wasteful as to take me, and let my training and talent lie fallow. I was told that God asks for ourselves and not for our talents because when He has us He has our talents too—obviously. The point of my offense was underscored, however, when Graham insisted that God *may* want to use me in some other capacity than my talents. I was a trained and useful church musician; let someone else lick stamps!

Next morning at the eucharist Graham asked me to start the dozen or so people off at a proper pitch for the offertory hymn; the chapel being too small for musical instruments, my perfect pitch was very handy for *a capella* singing. That morning I was completely unable to find a suitable pitch and the congregation valiantly struggled to follow my lead several times. I gave up in embarrassment. Suddenly I had lost the professional edge of my musicianship.

The next day it all came back again—after I had learned my lesson. Some people come to God clinging to their wealth; some come clinging to spiritual gifts; I had come clinging to my talent. He was not asking me to throw away my talent; He required only that I give it to Him so He could control it.

The lesson I learned? God needs servants who will obey Him, not specialists to advise Him.

A Law Student

When I first heard about Shirley's leukemia I was going through a sophomoric agnosticism, a time of hardness and judgment against my parent's religion. Life for me was brittle. My days were filled with the business of being a law student and I was lonely.

The news of Shirley brought to memory sunnier moments when we were classmates in high school. She was one of the popular ones and I found her attractive—perhaps a little beyond my reach—but I never tested it because she dated the same boy the entire time I knew her. None of her features were particularly outstanding but the overall impression was

72

a full-blossomed, dark-haired beauty that was neither just pretty nor sensuous; she was wholesome and lovely.

Shirley had more than usual talent. We both sang in the school choir and once when her first choice of recital accompanists fell through, she asked me to fill in. A professional sounding voice had won for her the lead role in our senior production of *Brigadoon,* in which she displayed an obvious inclination for the stage; and at the time of graduation her classmates voted her the "Most Talented Girl."

I decided to phone and offer my sympathy. To my surprise she sounded well, not anything like a person facing death, so I suggested a dinner date and she accepted.

A few nights later we spent nervous after-dinner hours together getting reacquainted. She avoided the subject of leukemia and I smoked two packs of cigarettes. But there was something about Shirley that intrigued me and I was unable to leave it alone. A few days later I called and arranged another date. That was the night that for some unknown reason I quit smoking.

On our second date Shirley told me a story relating recent events that were unlike anything I had ever heard before. She said God had healed her miraculously.

When I had heard the details of her professed healing, something in me was torn. I had thought supernatural things were nonsense, and this was more nonsense than a reasonable man could accept, but I half-believed it.

It all began when she blacked out while driving, barely avoiding a serious accident. A thorough physical examination revealed certain blood irregularities and further tests were made. Then a bone marrow sample was drawn from her sternum through a long, frightening needle. She had acute leukemia that could be expected to squeeze out her life within six weeks to two months.

Her parents were grief-stricken, but when news of the dreaded diagnosis was announced, Shirley's immediate response was to remember a hymn learned in childhood. She was in a ward at the cancer hospital surrounded by sickening

73

evidence of disease and death, but, strangely unperturbed, her mind was occupied with humming a tune, "Thank you Lord for saving my soul; Thank you Lord for making me whole. . . ."

In the wake of this shocking news, Shirley and her family encountered some Christians who believed in faith healing. Hopefully she submitted to their prayers. But at first nothing stopped the cancerous progression—neither prayer nor advanced chemotherapy—and after a frantic six weeks she was admitted to the hospital in the terminal stages of leukemia. Daily her life waned until she lay helpless and weak with intravenous needles in both arms, one supplying blood, the other drugs. It seemed her life was finished. One night when nauseated she awakened and lay helpless in her own vomit, reviewing the past few years of her life. She was a Christian, but there was little doubt her commitment had been shallow. Something happened in her soul that night, and while she was trapped in meditation a conviction of pride crept across her mind and humbly she submitted to the magnitude of God's loving forgiveness.

Her faith healing friends were persistent. There was a conference being held a few hundred miles from Houston and they were convinced she should attend; but her doctors were fearful that if she traveled that distance she would not return alive. Shirley was irresistibly drawn by the testimony of these friends, so she went to the conference and stayed several days. She was prayed for and was baptized with the Spirit. Her strength improved immediately.

Although she had left the hospital against medical advice, she returned to her doctors after the conference and they discovered that the advance of the disease had stopped dead in its tracks. According to them her leukemia was in a state of remission that might last a few months or a year at best, but she and her friends believed she was healed and there was great rejoicing.

My sympathetic phone call was made a month after Shirley had been released from the hospital. Her blood count was almost normal and she was a picture of health.

My world changed. We fell in love and were engaged to be married at the end of January during my semester break. The appearance of Shirley's health convinced us all that she was healed, and our families endorsed the marriage plans whole-heartedly. Her friends who had taken her to the healing conference were dubious: "Could a believer be yoked to an unbeliever?" they seemed to say.

Three weeks before our wedding Shirley was readmitted to the hospital with an apparent relapse. The doctors prescribed experimental chemotherapy in an attempt to halt the fresh advance of abnormal white cells; but her system reacted violently to new drugs and her health's rapid deterioration spiraled into a vicious circle of potent medications and pain-ful side effects. The faith healing friends declared she had "lost her healing" because of disobedience to the word of scripture: she intended to marry an unbeliever. I was enraged at what to me was their arrogance and pettiness. I gathered from their many conversations with Shirley that they had hoped her miraculously restored life would be dedicated to witnessing to the pentecostal power of God. Her infatuation with me was a distraction and God had withdrawn His miracle.

Although little was said to me about it, I watched Shirley struggle through a very difficult decision. Much of her spiri-tual experience and the only hope of healing she had found were tied up with these friends, but her heart's desire was tied up with me. Within a week of our wedding she decided in my favor.

In the next few days the doctors discovered an effective medication that was without complications and Shirley was scheduled for release in time for the wedding. As it turned out, she relinquished her sick bed just long enough to partici-pate in the rehearsal, and returned the next day with a temperature of 103 degrees. Shortly after lunch an odd-

75

looking, cheerful stranger approached me asking if he might pray for Shirley. Willing to try anyone's medicine I bowed my head. No sooner had the man gone than a nurse arrived to check Shirley's temperature again—it was normal. The wedding was on!

My amazement at witnessing this small miracle—how else could it be explained?—was lost for a while in the flurry of festivities. We had planned an impressive candlelight ceremony with seven bridal attendants and guest artists providing the wedding music. I saw another miracle in the stamina that Shirley displayed throughout the lengthy affair. The next morning as an out-patient at the hospital she received her medication under a new surname.

The new medication checked the disease's advancement, enabling us to begin our married life as a normal couple. Shirley looked at home and natural performing the ordinary chores required by life in a small apartment. Somehow I managed to pass my first semester exams amid the upheaval caused by Shirley's illness just prior to our wedding, and now at the beginning of the new term my classes were arranged so I could take her for treatments three times a week. She was radiant and my love for her grew deeper each day.

When there was time to mull things over quietly, I began wondering about the miracles that happened on our wedding day. Gradually this musing became a serious question, an honest inquiry into her grace and self-assurance. With instinctive wisdom she made little attempt to win me with words when I asked about their source, but she suggested we investigate the move of the Spirit in an Episcopal church across town.

We arrived at Church of the Redeemer one Friday after their evening meeting had begun. The atmosphere was different from other pentecostal-type meetings she had taken me to. During the service there were spontaneous ministries of charismatic gifts and things went at a leisurely pace with occasional short periods of quiet—not fidgety silences, but

76

living moments of freedom and love. At the evening's conclusion there was a smaller meeting in the chapel for those with special prayer requests, and since Shirley had been visibly strengthened by the first part of the meeting she said she wanted to attend. The chapel was filled with fifty or sixty people whose unaccompanied voices saturated the air with a glorious sound. We were impressed with a keen sense of expectancy surrounding the men ministering to those who came forward one after another with their requests. Shirley went forward and at the pastor's urging related to the congregation a conversation they had had in his office that week; she disclosed a simple but very helpful revelation.

For about six months she had been confused. On the advice of those who believed she was physically healed, she had begun to anticipate that the eventual accomplishment of the miracle would be a testimony to Houston churches, many of which rejected spiritual healing. She had been exhorted not to look at the empirical evidence of her disease but to the promises of God. If Shirley could state with her lips that she had been healed when there were still obvious symptoms, she would be showing a strong faith. God would vindicate that by the eventual fact of her healing.

Of course Shirley wanted to be healed, and she had asked God to do so. But the promise he had quickened to her mind at the moment of the leukemia diagnosis was a word of simple assurance in His power to draw her to Himself. On others' advice she had tried to claim a healing, but the attempt felt less than honest. She was caught between dishonesty and faithlessness when she wanted neither; hence the confusion.

The counsel she had more recently received settled her mind about faith. Her assurance from God was that whether in life or in death Christ was glorified in her and He was the savior of her soul; she need claim nothing in faith more or less than that—her health was in the hand of God's mercy.

I received comfort from hearing Graham Pulkingham's

advice. In the days that followed I began hungering for God, to know Him in the same intimate way Shirley did. The example of her life and the startling events surrounding our wedding were drawing me back into the presence of the living God.

Shirley's experience of baptism with the Spirit and speaking in tongues was foreign to me, but if a similar experience could bring peace and joy to my restless heart I wanted it. For the first time in years I confessed the Lordship of Jesus and then asked to be baptized with the Spirit.

The answer came a few days later through the prayer of a guest minister at a home meeting. What he prayed for is lost from memory, but what I received was joy. When the man encouraged me into the gift of tongues I battled my self-consciousness as he assured me there were words on the tip of my tongue. Managing to imitate some of his unusual sounds I made a tentative beginning that developed into a flow of unintelligible syllables. I left the room speaking in tongues.

Suddenly I too was a charismatic enthusiast. Shirley's fervent prayers for me had been answered and a new unity strengthened our relationship. I discovered for myself the source of her radiance.

Three weeks after my baptism in the Spirit, Shirley was again hospitalized with a high fever. It was Friday and I went to the prayer meeting at Church of the Redeemer to solicit their prayers. Her fever vanished in the night. But while we rejoiced some disappointing news came: the doctors were keeping her there for observation. The cancerous white cells, once again developing immunity to current medications, had multiplied rapidly and the research staff must find a new drug. One experiment after another failed and Shirley's body was at the mercy of its destructive foe.

The days of that period of hospitalization were for me a physical and emotional marathon. I managed to bear up under the weight of my other commitments, but the only thing that really mattered was Shirley. A losing battle with leukemia became the preoccupation of our lives as we whirled together in a kaleidoscope of thoughts and feelings that were usually intense and often perplexing.

Shirley had been in the hospital for about a month when Graham Pulkingham phoned saying he wanted to talk with me as soon as possible. The call was a surprise; I was neither a member of his church nor a frequenter of their prayer meetings. We agreed to meet in his office one day after my classes at the university. On the way to the appointment my thoughts reviewed other times I had been at the church—there were only four or five of them—and each time it had felt very much like home. I was especially comfortable with the pastor; his peaceful, strong personality put me at ease. The previous week he had surprised me with an embrace, saying I was a person for whom the Lord had given him a special kind of love. The perplexities of life were eased and I found strength and encouragement in that moment.

When I reached the church he was awaiting in his office and we greeted each other in an exchange of pleasantries. Offering me a chair he arranged one for himself facing me. Plainly there was something serious to be said.

"Bill," he began, "there are people in the parish who keep up with Shirley's condition, you know, and last Friday at the chapel service a woman told us how bleak things are right now. She asked us to take a stand of faith with Shirley's friends who believe God will raise her up and restore her to health. That caused a little confusion in me, Bill, because I wasn't sure what the Lord wanted. It's God's mercy that I trust. If He gives me a special nudge about Shirley's healing I'll gladly speak about that. But in the absence of a special word I can only trust His mercy."

I assured him I knew the confusion because I'd been in the middle of it for a month.

"I thought it was time to face the confusion head on, Bill, so I suggested that everyone who could, begin fasting and ask the Lord to clear the air a bit. I wanted to know *how* to pray for Shirley. About forty of us started fasting last Saturday morning and we kept it up till Monday."

Graham's voice was soft and he spoke slowly, picking his words. He was looking me full in the face.

"There's a woman in St. Louis named Kathleen Thomerson," he continued. "She played the organ here for a while last summer and got baptized with the Spirit at the same time.

"Last Monday she called me and her first words were, 'Graham are you fasting?' You can imagine my surprise. For a couple of days she'd been having strange thoughts and turning up unusual scriptures, but she didn't want to be misled so she asked the Lord somehow to show her if they weren't reliable. When she asked for a sign He indicated we were fasting, so she decided to call me and find out."

I began sensing the gravity of Graham's words.

"When I told her to go ahead, she said she'd been praying last Friday and Saturday and kept remembering scriptures about the way God is glorified by death. She mentioned several places in the Bible, like the death of Lazarus and Stephen's stoning—other places, too. When she felt an urge to share these scriptures with me she couldn't understand why, so she prayed some more, and on Sunday something pretty positive happened. Mind you, she doesn't know you or Shirley, Bill, but the Lord gave her the name Shirley—sort of out of the blue."

Graham leaned forward and put his hand on my knee. The tone of his voice was earnest but gentle. "Bill, I don't know how to say this except straight out. The Lord told Kathleen we were praying for Shirley's healing, but He wants us to release her to Him so He can take her home."

The words my heart feared had been spoken.

For a few breathless seconds my eyes were fixed on Graham's face. Then suddenly I felt the emotional impact of what he had been saying and it was as if Shirley were already

80

gone. Tears of grief poured down my face. Graham moved close and I clung to him for a very long time, heaving and sobbing.

The tears finally quit and Graham asked quietly, "Bill, do you think you should tell Shirley?"

At the sound of her name I had to choke back tears. I shook my head No.

Graham took my hand and pressed it against his cheek. "Why don't you find a place where you can be alone," he said. "Tell the Lord how it hurts."

Rubbing my swollen eyes I answered, "I'll have plenty of time to pray while I'm driving across town."

Outside the church I wept again. Going quickly to the privacy of my car I wept with a lonely mourning and agonized before God. *Why, Lord, why?*

"He wants us to release her . . . take her home." Words that rang true—but impossible to contemplate!

When the first shock of Graham's words passed, confusion was gone too; for the first time in weeks I found a measure of peace. And for a while there was genuine gladness I could serve my sick wife with the same grace and tenderness which I had felt from her during the days of my agnostic hardness.

But soon confusion set in again. Some friends redoubled their efforts at building our hope to the level of their faith. About two weeks after my conversation with Graham, I came to the point of rationalizing what the Lord had said about wanting to take Shirley to Himself. Perhaps what He really wanted was for me just to be willing to release her.

Shirley's parents and I wanted her to live as much as our faith healing friends did, so we considered a visit to Kathryn Kuhlman, but instead summoned a minister from out of state. She had a proven ministry of healing and we decided to trust her wisdom. After seeing Shirley alone, and praying with her, the woman announced that God had told her these facts: If I would demonstrate blind faith in the Bible's promises to heal, and take Shirley off her medicines and home from the hospital, she would improve daily and be healed quickly.

I felt impaled on the horns of an intolerable dilemma. If there was even a remote chance that Shirley's healing depended on removing her from the hospital, how could I ever live with myself if we didn't obey? But she was so helplessly sick and in constant need of pain killers. Her blood count had reached an all-time low and because her veins were collapsed the doctors had inserted a permanent tube into her leg, which meant confinement to a bed.

Against strong protests from the doctors we took Shirley home to her parents' house. Day by day her condition worsened, though we had been told it would improve. Deprived of proper care she rapidly lost ground and her suffering increased. On the fourth frantic day I received a phone call from Graham. He and a friend wanted to come by the house for a visit.

When they arrived that evening his friend visited with Shirley's parents in the kitchen while Graham talked with us in Shirley's bedroom. He was quiet but insistent.

"Shirley, has God Himself told you plainly that He's going to heal you?"

Shirley hesitated and we looked at each other. Then slowly she began shaking her head No.

"What about you, Bill?"

I held back tears and reached across the bed for Shirley's hand. She was in such pain. Wearily I answered, "I guess not."

"What *has* the Lord said to you Shirley?"

She hesitated again, then looking at me said in quiet confidence, "That He loves me—that He died for my sin—that He's merciful—that I can trust Him."

Graham smiled kindly. "That's wonderful. It doesn't mean that He won't heal you, Shirley, but as far as I can see it's not your testimony that He said He would. Others seem to think they hear that—and that's fine for them—but your faith has

82

to rest on what the Lord's said to you, not on what He's said to someone else.

"Bill, if you knew that God intended simply to be merciful and loving, if there was even a chance He wasn't going to heal Shirley of leukemia, would you be doing anything different than you are now?"

My answer came without hesitation. "Yes, I'd have her back in the hospital where she could be comfortable."

"Amen," murmured Graham's friend from the foot of Shirley's bed where he had quietly posted himself after entering the room.

The hospital officials graciously readmitted Shirley the next day but the advance of her disease was irreversible. We were all helpless, and the swarm of her many counselors thinned to an infrequent straggler. Now there were round-the-clock tender ministrations from our families and from the nursing staff; and there were quiet night-time hours of silent sharing between Shirley and me—often spent to the rhythm of her fitful slumbers—when in the darkness of a semiprivate hospital room we knew a communion of our love as deep as any that had ever gone before.

She had been readmitted on a Friday. The weekend was a parade of hospital routine, blood transfusions and new experimental drugs: though the progress of Shirley's pain and weakness had settled into a plateau, there were no signs of improvement.

Graham had asked for daily reports and on Monday when I called he said, "Bill, do you spend your nights at the apartment?"

"Yes, some of them," I said. "I don't get there till twelve, though, maybe one or two. It all depends on when Shirley gets to sleep. Why?"

"Oh I wanted to spend some time with you but I knew you were at the hospital most of the time. I don't want to be in your way. Maybe there's no time right now, huh?"

"Well, if you come by the apartment around one o'clock

I'll probably be there. But isn't that pretty late for you?"

"No. As a matter of fact I thought of staying up all night to pray. I don't mean you would have to stay up—would it bother you if I were there? I just want to be with you for a while."

"I don't think so," I said, feeling a bit dubious. "I've never stayed up all night praying. But come on—if I get tired I'll go to bed."

"Tonight?"

"OK, see you then."

Almost every night for two long months I had returned to an empty apartment. Graham arrived shortly after me that night, and his presence was a welcome change. But it was more than just a change. I don't recall that anything very significant was said or that we did anything unusual—at about four o'clock I fell sound asleep—yet somehow that night the mysteries of our two lives were fused together in the mercy of Christ's compassion. Graham had not come to give counsel; he was there simply because he loved me.

Early the next morning Graham went with me to the hospital for a visit with Shirley. She was in an oxygen tent; during the night her breathing had become very labored and she was much weaker.

Wednesday at noon I called Graham to say that Shirley was in and out of a coma, her consciousness was more and more scattered, and things looked bad. He told me of a chapel in an Episcopal hospital across the street and suggested I spend time there in prayer. Before leaving I stood at the foot of Shirley's bed at a moment when she was coming around; when her eyes opened I was at the focus of her confused vision. She sat up, extended her arm toward me and called my name. After I smiled and touched her, she settled back into a quiet sleep and I left for the chapel.

Now Shirley sleeps the quiet sleep of those who rest in Jesus. He took her while I was praying in a lonely chapel. The page system had announced my name in the distance and I was warned of something. The rest was told by the strong arms and unashamed tears of my father, whom I met coming across the street to get me.

Having steeled myself against that moment, to begin with I walked numbly among the many things the bereaved accomplish in a merciful state of shock. Sometime during the afternoon I called Graham. He asked to see me as soon as things settled down and late that evening we met in his office. In the fold of his arms everything of my grief that was angry and frustrated and hurt was touched by his prayer and saw beginning hope of release. I wept the bitterest of tears and mourned the loss of the only person I had ever opened my soul to.

God glorified Himself in the death of Shirley DeSoto Farra on May 25, 1966, three weeks before I moved into the rectory of Church of the Redeemer and became a member of a growing charismatic community there. In Graham's household the hideous pain of separation from my wife of four months began slowly to be succored. It was not easy at times. There were moments when I felt I had been duped by God. He enticed me from my agnosticism into the warmth and freedom of an exquisite relationship with one of His loveliest lambs. Then He withdrew her from my life leaving a naked relationship with Him. But it was not disembodied, I was to learn. I found the Jesus of my wife's soul embodied in a community of His servants gathered at Redeemer Church, and I joined Him there.

the
ministry

As he finished the last chapter of *Gathered for Power* my wife's brother commented to his mother, "That's great, but when's the other shoe going to drop?" He was left with a sense of anticipation because my first book only hinted at the details of renewal in Redeemer Church.

So far in this book I have attempted to widen the perspective, to bring the story a step or two farther along, and to introduce more of the *dramatis personae* who approached center stage during act one of the saga. Before Redeemer Church itself could become a strong charismatic parish, the two visionary aspects of its renewed beginnings—intercessory power in neighborhood ministry and communal life in the church—had to join forces and share a common grace and calling. That began happening in the summer of 1965 when community members—some by intentional commitment, others out of desperate need—moved their lives lock, stock and barrel into the declining Eastwood neighborhood. A survey of the events that followed constitutes dropping the other shoe.

Chapter VI

There is a story about medical corps hardships in the trenches during World War I, when often even major surgery was attempted by squeamish corpsmen in an effort to salvage otherwise perishing lives.

Once an unconscious soldier's leg, nearly severed above the knee by a piece of heavy shrapnel, had to be removed without the aid of anesthetic; his unconscious state was an advantage. The inexperienced medic stationed a corporal at the patient's shoulders in case consciousness should return at an inconvenient moment; the limb was then hacked off with a blunt knife. The corporal blanched with nausea. In an attempt to draw his attention from the gore, the medic asked pointlessly, "Hey, up at that end, how's the patient?" the corporal replied, "I don't know how he is at your end, Sarge, but he shore acts dead up here."

During the first half of 1963, it was as Christ's lonely servant, He whetted my appetite to see charismatic gifts of the Spirit at work in a ministry of intercession. By the time a peek into the future communalism of Redeemer Church had been given, I interpreted the vision to be hinting at an eventual conglomeration of individuals, each with one or more charismatic gifts for healing, deliverance, reconciliation, miraculous faith, and so on. Immediately after my baptism with the Spirit, these very gifts appeared as ministering "tools" in the personal intercessory work I was then engaged in, but the effective outreach of their powers was strangely selective. In addition, a spiritual melee came following in their wake because these particular gifts—joined now by the tintinnabulous sound of tongues—were crowd gatherers. When the dusts of this confusion had settled, thirty-three of us became wedded in the very fiber of our lives and a growing community was underway. However, not every member exercised the gifts I had originally presumed, and there were charisms developing whose existence until then was merely suspected. Looking back I could see that if the community had developed as anticipated, its effectiveness for parochial renewal would have been much like the medic's attempt to salvage a limb of the soldier's corpse. God had not given me a vision for, nor was He primarily designing, an "outreach" ministry; He was about the business of building a corporate community, a full and healthy body of Christ in the institutional forms of Redeemer Church in Houston's Eastwood section. I knew that, in my mind's eye. During 1965 I began to see it in the parish neighborhood.

God is not so capricious as to make silk purses out of sows' ears—unless, of course, there are no silkworms on hand. In 1963 I was an *ingenue* about charismatic community matters; by 1964 I was little better than an *arriviste*. But by 1965 I was learning that before the Spirit of God actually erects a corporate community of the body of Christ, He gathers together a force of community builders much as general contractors engage artisans to construct a house. Some of the thirty-three who moved into the parish neighborhood bore charisms for building the community. They were men and women whose natural endowments were enhanced by these spiritual gifts—persons whose vision, administrative and leadership ability had already been proven.

Until community members began bringing their whole lives into the neighborhood and taking up residence there, I had supposed the renewed parish would be a colony of committed Christians. I imagined them banded together for mutual support and protection, occasionally foraying out into the wicked neighborhood to rescue souls, a few at a time. That was not how it happened. To begin with, very few neighborhood people associated themselves with the nascent charismatic community, but neighborhood-type people—the poor from elsewhere—responded in great enough numbers to keep the rest of us hopping. Also, the concentration of God's power was in the community, not in the neighborhood; the poor were being effectively reached, but only as they entered into a shared life with us in the community. Like the professional and business people whose imaginations had been captured by a life-style healing community, so the poor were moving into the neighborhood. But somehow these poor had been converted to a better sense of caring and stewardship— for everything, including one another—than they themselves had known before we shared our lives with them. The charismatic community was reversing the movement of social patterns from the inner city to the suburbs. As one after another community member occupied a residence in the parish neighborhood, a five-block radius around the church began visibly to brighten. Neighboring property owners saw the changes and suddenly paint was applied, grass and flowers were planted, shrubbery was trimmed and tended. The face of Redeemer's immediate neighborhood was losing its appearance of blight.

Very quickly the community building charisms became closely defined. I hesitate to name them because they have been household items in every novel ecclesiastical system imaginable, but by us they were cherished as the most superb gifts of all—for the purpose of God's design in Eastwood. They were Paul's list of Christ's graces recorded in the fourth chapter of Ephesians: apostles, prophets, evangelists, pastors and teachers. We found these not to be "offices" or "persons," but forces afoot among community members, power at work to convert and nurture and strengthen, to keep peace alive and love foremost, to build up in truth while guarding against harmful infringements, to govern and guide, to increase, correct, and encourage.

These gifts were in stewardship to a few of us, but under the supervision of three: the doctor, the lawyer, and myself. We were assisted by the engineer, the laborer, our five wives, and the editor. In addition to sharing life fully with the rest of the growing community we were together another three to five hours a day—praying, sharing in God's word, discussing, listening, serving, encouraging, and loving one another. We had received a baptism with Christ's love and a commission to care for His little flock in Eastwood. Knowing the stuff of our authority in carrying out that commission to be purity and fervency of love for one another, we were determined that literally nothing short of death would cause us to forsake our calling. We had the profoundest respect for the Savior in one another. Each man's soul was a hallowed garden of treasures where we were privileged to walk in the day's coolness together with the Father of every good and perfect gift. Hesitant to contradict, coerce or offend, tender in loving concern, without accusation or mistrust, we experienced an unspeakable dimension of sacramental love, beholding Christ in one another's faces. What a paltry sum to pay for so priceless a pearl!

The community was stable and grew daily. The sick were healed, the bound were loosed, the blind saw, the lame walked, the dead were raised, and the gospel was preached to the poor—in the community where God had drawn us and was loving all of us into new dimensions of life.

Chapter VII

Sometimes the word of God stands out in neon-splendored relief against our drab surroundings. That was my wife, Betty's, first impression when she entered Redeemer Church to worship. It was not only that the church had no windows: its curved, cavernous design forced her eye to a dossal figure of Christ ascending in a cascade of brilliant clouds and surrounded by a throng of enraptured worshipers. In some ways that was good. But Christ and His wall-paint friends were bathed in light, while the warm bodies of living congregations could barely be seen in the dimly lit church. Over the years a gradual loss of efficiency in irreplaceable neon tubing, the nave's only light source, had caused a sixty percent diminishment of vision. Because it had been gradual, only visitors were struck with a sudden sense of blindness and commented about it.

Was that perhaps a providential description of this once vital inner city church? A gradual loss of power seen only by outsiders until decrepitude had set in!

By mid-1964 it was more the rigor of death than the waste of decrepitude that had set in. The institutional forms of Redeemer Church were by then alive in name only. Without interruption since the day of my arrival in September 1963 I had continued to hold Sunday services and one weekday eucharist, but everything else—the choir, vestry, men's and women's organizations, Sunday school—was subjected to continual change and either ceased to function or wandered weakly for several years without effective leadership. On the

94

other hand the volunteer community where my heart's fancy was, and which had sprouted on the old parish's gravesite, was by 1966 on the verge of full bloom: its appearance was very much like a church. The word of God, so obviously at the heart of the community's self-awareness, was more splendid there in brilliance than the mural's message compared to the drab parish church.

Slowly over months of growth the community had developed for itself a functional structure of leadership and a spontaneous freedom in worship. The leadership was utterly devoid of division between "lay" and "ordained" except on the ground of sacramental function. In fact, the minister (singular) was literally the whole community of men and women; where we lived and the sorts of persons attempting to live out their lives together in a circumstance of intense sharing made this a necessity for survival. Yet there was a structure: our lives were ordered on the principle of submission one to another in love, and we functioned according to a faith that God would enable certain members with the necessary charismatic gifts for efficient work and effective leadership. Pastoral care, outreach in evangelism, prophetic visions and utterances, teaching authority, services among the brethren, administrative responsibility, all were the property of the whole community and could be exercised by every member in varying degrees and with more or less frequency according to the person's maturity, availability, and charisms. These were called ministries and were under the governmental oversight of a group of men whom we called "elders" simply as a means of identification. These were not officials; they were elders in the sense that a community looked to them for oversight because their charism was "to oversee" and the whole community readily assented to the fact.

Finally, in late 1966 the community had been proved as a place to mature the lives of those walking in the Spirit and to perfect every kind of ministry. Then over the months of 1967 the entire staff and leadership of the dormant parish was slowly infiltrated by men and women trained and perfected in ministry through their life in the community and, suddenly, there was an upsurge of support and new life in the parish itself. The dual vision of parish as life-style community, and of ministry as sacrificial intercession, was being imparted to the parish and by the end of 1968 when the task was finished the community disappeared. In its place was an entirely renewed and reformed Church of the Redeemer: charismatic in ministry, corporate in life and leadership, sacrificial in loving service, and eucharistic to its core—a flavor not possible until the parish and community had become one.

Parallel to the evolution of new and charismatic structures of ministry was a development of freedom and freshness in worship. This unique and remarkable charism began with a very loud word from the Lord to Betty Pulkingham.

It would be difficult to say how much the obscured interior of Redeemer Church had to do with the miserable quality of worship that Betty experienced there in 1963, but both darkness of vision and rigidity of ritual were offensively there, like misery and its company. The situation was epitomized in a comical contrast between sounds made by trained operatic choir hirelings and the apologetic mutterings of the congregation. Betty was sickened by it; she was all too familiar with professionalism in worship. Having sung in one of the finest church choirs in the southwest at St. David's, Austin, she had been excited by the musical excellence displayed there in every anthem and hymn, then saddened and hurt when the paid singers spent the sermon time reading paperbacks that had been slipped into their choir folders before the service. It was a mockery, but at least the music was excellent. Here at Redeemer Church it was ludicrous.

In this grey place, with these grey sounds, surrounded by what looked like grey people, the Spirit of God troubled the waters of her soul and fairly shouted the command: *"Let every thing that hath breath praise the Lord!!!"* From that

96

moment on, Betty had a vision of the Church of the Redeemer peopled by worshipers who were alive to a spirit of praise. At the beginning, she knew little of what this would involve, but God's desire for a praise-filled people gripped her soul.

Stage one in her plan took place in the small downstairs chapel where so much had already transpired and where community members, freshly endued with the Spirit's empowering baptism, began to meet in 1964. The first order of business was a worshiping community. Some, like Dr. Bob Eckert and Jerry Barker, a lawyer, still lived forty-odd miles away, and 5:30 in the morning was a popular daily hour for praise and prayer gatherings before the workday began. By the summer of 1965 when several families moved into the neighborhood of the church, whole households were assembling for evening prayers and fellowship together. Tuesday and Friday nights after the public prayer meeting, many worshipers stayed on for a trek to the chapel where elders prayed individually for those who approached the altar rail. Elbow to elbow in this small resonant chamber with friends in Christ, we began intimately to experience the awesomeness of God's presence with His people. It really was awesomely true in that place that God inhabited the praises of His people: He was almost tangibly there—to speak, to heal, to deliver, to comfort, to meet us in whatever our need or desire might be. It was an entirely new dimension of faith and worship for all of us to see people healed in the midst of our spontaneous praises.

As a boiling pot of stew blends its various ingredients and wafts a mouth-watering aroma through the whole house, so it is with a Christian community truly at worship: the varied and intricate beauty of its life is pervasive. Our worship in the chapel began to have a rich aroma and there developed a gentleness to the singing—sometimes peaceful and soft, sometimes bright and rhythmic. The chapel was too small to accommodate a piano or organ, so the Lord encouraged us to trust Him for starting songs at a good pitch, in a comfortable tempo, without the obvious leadership of a "musician." He taught us how to listen to one another when we sang, without trying to out-sing our neighbor. He taught us to sing simply, bright little unison choruses like "I am so glad that Jesus loves me"; and He taught us to sing boldly some of the greatest hymns of Christendom such as "Alleluia! Sing to Jesus" (*Hyfrydol*) with four parts and a descant soaring out on top! And He taught us to sing in the Spirit without the use of any known song at all. He taught us; we sat at His feet; we worshiped Him.

In the spring of 1965 the vestry cut the parish budget and removed every item under the music column. That was in part an act of faith: surely God could raise up His own ministers. I suppose in the mind of some of us there was always the possibility that Betty, a competent choir director and keyboard instrumentalist, could pinch-hit if necessary. But Betty was expecting our fifth baby; she was incapacitated until sometime after June. The axe was laid to the root of the tree. When the choir gathered in the narthex on the Sunday before the vestry's decision was to go into effect, there were restless whisperings among several of the faithful sopranos. Finally one of them, flushed and agitated, turned and asked Betty, "And what, pray tell, are we going to do for an organist next Sunday? Mr. —— says this is the last time he will play." The silence caused by the question was deep, but so was the assurance of faith when Betty answered, "I don't know, but I know God will send someone."

He did. The someone He sent was worshipping in the congregation the next Sunday while the organ bench was occupied by an organist friend of Arabella's, a University of Texas graduate who was passing through Houston for a short visit. The someone's name was Kathleen Thomerson, a one-time student of Betty's in the Music Department at Texas University. Kathleen had gone on to achieve great success and recognition as a concert and church organist. She was a musician's musician, in town for the summer while her husband looked for a teaching position in his field of graduate study.

Kathleen sought out Betty after the service and they got reacquainted. Then Kathleen said, "I wonder if it would be convenient for me to practice on your organ some during the summer, Betty. I have several recitals coming up in the fall, and I don't want to get rusty."

"Why, yes, I'm sure we can work something out. We'd love for you to practice here." Betty was relishing the thought of it. "You know, it's been years since I heard you play. I may be tempted to leave my housework and sneak over and listen!"

"Great! Oh ... and if you need a supply organist this summer—I mean, when your organist goes on vacation I'd be glad to help out."

Her words re-echoed. "I'd be glad to ... if you need ... !"

The Lord did it, and in the nick of time. Kathleen was not just any organist. She was the very finest church musician imaginable. Betty was at first stunned by the magnificence of God's provision and then her heart leaped in praise. *The Lord sent us an organist! Did you hear that, world? Did you hear that, trees and shrubs? Did you hear that, cows and horses and creeping things? Did you hear that, sun and moon? Did you hear that, sons of God? He sent us his organist! Hallelujah!"*

After Kathleen moved to St. Louis in September, Betty took over as choir director and organist, and during the next year the choir began to increase in numbers under her leadership. It was an unusual choir. Few of its twenty members had any musical training, but they had one thing many church choirs lack: a sense of calling to worship God with their whole being as a commitment in ministry. Choir membership was regarded as a community service to the parish. Because of this depth of commitment God was able to take these meager skills and magnify them out of all proportion to what each singer individually presented Him. As the congregation gathered for worship Sunday after Sunday, everyone felt loved by God Himself when the choir sang. Not only that, the congregation began to respond by entering in: the parish was beginning to develop a sense of corporate worship!

By the summer of 1966 the choir was established in a real sense of its purpose and calling. Kathleen returned for a second summer at the organ bench and Betty, continuing as choir director, saw in a vision the next step in raising up a praise-filled people. It was described in II Chronicles 5:13-14: "It came even to pass, as the trumpeters and singers were as *one*, to make *one* sound to be heard in praising and thanking the Lord; and when they lifted up their voice with the trumpets and cymbals and instruments of music, and praised the Lord, saying, For he is good; for his mercy endureth forever: that then the house was filled with a cloud, even the house of the Lord; so that the priests could not stand to minister by reason of the cloud: for the glory of the Lord had filled the house of God."

This picture of the unity of God's people and of God's house filled with His glory was confirmed in the form of a vision received by a faithful woman during a Sunday eucharist that summer. Sharing it with me later, she described what she saw as "the church crammed full of people, people even filling the balcony, all of them raising their hands and praising God." Such a sight had certainly not been seen in Redeemer Church before. During my first months there I used to wonder what the designer had in mind when he drew plans for a nave that could seat a thousand people. The two hundred souls who then made up the congregation rattled around like peas in a pod. But now God was speaking to us about His desires to fill His people with His praise and to fill that place with His people. At the time it was almost impossible to imagine.

During her second summer in Houston, Kathleen Thomerson added another touch to the power of God's praises among us: a gift for new song. Her musical imagination was

100

full of toccatas and fugues and beautiful, complex music. It suddenly struck her there seemed to be no room for simple songs of faith and praise, of the kind Paul exhorted the saints to continue in. She asked the Lord to change that. On the morning of July 4th she woke up with a new tune humming around in her head, and the words, "I love the name of Jesus, King of my heart; He is everything to me." A song had been born.

More than that. An anointing for new songs had come to rest upon a body of believers. In the years to come, we were to look back at "I love the name of Jesus" as the lock that opened the dam and let waters of creativity roll in. For the Lord began to express Himself in many new songs of fellowship. Most of them just "happened" in the midst of our prayer and praise in the chapel—or at a later date, during the eucharist. Few were ever written down before being sung, and some not for a long time after. The Lord was pouring out a gift of music on His beloved people.

By the end of 1967 a very special homemade stew was being savored. It turned out to be a tantalizing gourmet delight whose aroma filled the house of the Lord. All aspects of parish life and ministry were by then under the guidance of community-trained leaders who brought a remarkable integrity of communalism to everything the Church of the Redeemer did. But somehow that integrity was intensified into a deeper unity of praise at the Sunday parish Eucharists; a unique flavor of music was giving character to the gathering together of God's people in Eastwood. It was a "people's" music, a *gebrauchmusik* of high order; and there was an exciting new charism associated with it, one that clearly testified with prophetic comfort: "This music is a gift for my praises upon this people."

1968 was a year of expansion: nothing new was added. Membership doubled, income increased a hundred percent, and nearby churches began to inquire into the source of our grace. The aroma of Redeemer Church's life and ministry had

101

seeped out of the doors into the streets; it was wafted on the breezes of renewal across Texas, then across the nation the next year. Soon it would find its way around the world.

The following year, 1969, a fresh force of evangelism moved powerfully across the face of the parish itself and . . .

But, then, that begins a whole new story that can wait for another time of telling.